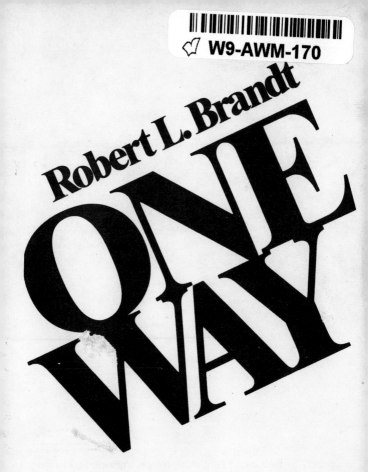

Robert L. Brandt

ONE WAY

Gospel Publishing House
Springfield Missouri

02-0909

© 1977 by the Gospel Publishing House, Springfield, Missouri
65802. Adapted from *Salvation* by G. Raymond Carlson, © 1963
by the Gospel Publishing House. All rights reserved.
Library of Congress Catalog Card Number 77-075601
International Standard Book Number 0-88243-909-X
Printed in the United States of America

A teacher's guide for group study with this book is available from
the Gospel Publishing House (order number 32-0179).

Contents

1

Scheme for Escape

"By the time I was thirty-five and had seen something of life, I, who'd been taught from earliest childhood by society and my family to be an atheist and materialist, was already one of those who cannot live without God. I am glad that it is so." That is the testimony of Svetlana Alliluyeva, daughter of Joseph Stalin, now living in the United States.

Escaping from Russia was not easy. But she did it. Here's how.

She had been married to an Indian named Brajesh Singh. After his death, Svetlana was permitted a trip to India where the ashes of her beloved husband would be cast into the Ganges.

While in India the possibility of escaping Russia began seeping into her thinking. At one point she came across some lines by Mahatma Gandhi which fanned the flame. "It is possible," he wrote, "for a single individual to defy the whole might of an unjust empire to save his honor, his religion, his soul, and lay the foundation for that empire's fall or its regeneration."

What she calls the "American Theme" began to fasten itself upon her. She indicates the idea grew progressively stronger as she pondered it. But how could it be done? How could she escape Russia and yet spare her children, residents in Russia, from awful reprisal? How could she bear leaving her homeland, her friends, and her family, and go to live the rest of her life in a faraway strange land?

Her little time in India had already answered the last question. There she had found such self-assurance, such calm, and such tranquility, though they were alien to her nature before.

Finally her decision was made. Her scheme for escape was beset with complications. Russian officials in India were anxious for her return to her homeland for she had already overstayed the original allotted time. When she thought of escape she knew her passport would likely be held, as was the custom, until she was at the airport ready for takeoff to Russia. However, upon hearing her announce her intention to return shortly, the responsible Russian official handed her the passport.

Time was of the essence. The moment came when she knew delay until the morrow might completely change her course. "Yes, it would be better to do it all in the evening," she wrote. "Why did I ever think of the morning? In the daytime everything would be seen; now it was getting dark, lights were few. Yes, it must happen today, at once; why was I putting it off? I must decide quickly. . . ."

After that, things happened fast. She had to thread her way past several obstacles. She was to have been picked up that evening and taken to dinner. She must leave before someone arrived to pick her up. Only minutes might separate the arrival of the taxi she had called and the other ride provided for her. Once in the taxi she must pass the Soviet Embassy —

a chance to take. And once in the American Embassy, what could she expect? Would they buy her story?

The taxi arrived first. The driver took a shortcut behind the Soviet Embassy. In a moment she was in the American Embassy, and her red-covered Soviet passport set the wheels in motion for her freedom.

Later she wrote: "The glass door of the American Embassy in Delhi was my entrance into the Western world. . . ."

What an ordeal! What a scheme! What an escape!

Could anything be worse than Communism's bondage? Aleksandr I. Solzhenitsyn's *The Gulag Archipelago*[1] makes you wonder all the more. And when someone escapes, you understand and secretly rejoice, hoping others will have the same success.

We fear Communism, and rightly so, but there is a worse monster. The Bible calls it sin.

Communism encompasses billions, making them slaves to the system, depriving them of human rights, oppressing many, imprisoning many, slaughtering many. Even so, it holds a poor second to sin. *On the test*

Sin makes a wider sweep. It affects every human, none excepted: "Wherefore, as by one man sin entered into the world, and death by sin; and so death passed upon all men, for that all have sinned" (Romans 5:12).

Sin leaves its victims naked: "And he said, I heard thy voice in the garden, and I was afraid, because I was naked; and I hid myself" (Genesis 3:10).

---

[1] Aleksandr I. Solzhenitsyn, *The Gulag Archipelago* (NY: Harper & Row Publishers, Inc., 1975).

7

Sin cuts us off from God's presence. "Therefore the Lord God sent him forth from the garden of Eden, to till the ground from whence he was taken. So he drove out the man" (vv. 23, 24).

Sin robs us of God's glory: "For all have sinned, and come short of the glory of God" (Romans 3:23).

Sin makes fugitives and vagabonds of us, leaving us lost: "A fugitive and a vagabond shalt thou be in the earth" (Genesis 4:12). "For the Son of man is come to seek and to save that which was lost" (Luke 19:10).

Sin makes men poor, breeds sorrow, makes captives, blinds and bruises, not only for time, but for ever. (See Luke 4:18.) "And sin, when it is finished, bringeth forth death" (James 1:15).

What to do about it? By clever scheming Svetlana Alliluyeva escaped Russia. Others have defected when the chance came. But sin, who can escape it? Nobody!

That doesn't mean men have not tried. Indeed they have. But always in vain. The first pair tried with fig-leaf aprons (Genesis 3:7), and with a hideout in the trees (v. 8). The first child born to human parents tried with a sacrifice of his own making (4:3). Since then men have never ceased trying, either by denying sin's existence, by some form of monastic solitude, by religion, by law, or by good deeds. Nothing has worked. Every effort or scheme has in the end been a total washout. You finally get the feeling it is like trying to invent perpetual motion.

"When all else fails, read the instructions." It is not that there is no effective scheme for escape. But, putting it plainly, only one is surefire. The Bible lays out the plan in detail. It explains the only plan that

8

works. There is no other way to escape sin or its fearful end. "How shall we escape, if we neglect so great salvation; which at the first began to be spoken by the Lord, and was confirmed unto us by them that heard him" (Hebrews 2:3).

Glutted Market

"The devil made me do it!" Who hasn't heard that line? Some horrible crimes have been excused that way. But the peddlers of false schemes always give God the "credit," whether it be Jehovah's Witnesses, Christian Scientists, Mormons, or Sun Myung Moon.

Though the market be glutted with a vast variety of do-it-yourself or we'll-do-it-for-you ideas for handling the sin problem, we had better not overlook the clear print of *the* instruction Book: "But though we, or an angel from heaven, preach any other gospel unto you than that which we have preached unto you, let him be accursed" (Galatians 1:8). "Neither is there salvation in any other: for there is none other name under heaven given among men, whereby we must be saved" (Acts 4:12).

Doing Our Own Thing

Sin is every man's problem, we say, but what is sin? Simply, sin is an act against God. The Ten Commandments show us this. Paul put it this way: "Nay, I had not known sin, but by the law" (Romans 7:7).

Sin is basically a relationship problem. Whatever separates man from God is sin. And sin is more a condition of the heart than an outward act. The act is the fruit of the condition. Sin is self against God. It got a stranglehold when Adam and Eve decided to please themselves instead of God (Genesis 3:6). Facing it squarely, sin is every man doing his own thing. The bad part is he is addicted; he can't quit. It is woven into the very fiber of his nature.

Solving the Problem

Man is a genius at solving his problems. That is why he has such a time admitting he can't solve the sin problem. But by now he should realize this.

It is pretty good advice when you can't solve your problem, to seek out someone who can. According to the Bible there is only One who can — God himself. The beautiful thing is, He has already done it!

God Became Man

That's a new wrinkle. There is nothing new about man trying to be God; that is how sin got started. But to get man out of his predicament, God decided to become a man. Don't think it was easy. The Bible says that though Jesus was "in the form of God, [He] thought it not robbery [a thing to be clung to] to be equal with God: but made himself of no reputation, and took upon him the form of a servant, and was made in the likeness of men: and being found in fashion as a man, he humbled himself, and became obedient unto death, even the death of the cross" (Philippians 2:6-8).

How did God become man and why? Let's find out why first. The Bible tells us: "For since by man came death, by man came also the resurrection of the dead" (1 Corinthians 15:21).

10

It is evident that since sin and death came by the act of a man, divine justice required that deliverance would also come by the act of a man. Romans 5 has a lot to say about this: "For if through the offense of one [man] many be dead, much more the grace of God, and the gift by grace, which is by one man, Jesus Christ, hath abounded unto many" (v. 15). "For as by one man's disobedience many were made sinners, so by the obedience of one [man] shall many be made righteous" (v. 19). (See also vv. 17, 18.)

God's scheme required a man, but not just any man. The man to do the job had to be sinless; otherwise, he would be unable to take the punishment for others' sins.

There was only one way to obtain such a man. God had to come out with an original—a man who was sinless. This required a relationship between a holy God and a virgin. Remember the angel's word to Mary: "The Holy Ghost shall come upon thee, and the power of the Highest shall overshadow thee: therefore also that holy thing which shall be born of thee shall be called the Son of God" (Luke 1:35).

Springing from this union was the God-man, Immanuel, the sinless One. "Behold, a virgin shall be with child, and shall bring forth a son, and they shall call his name Immanuel, which being interpreted is, God with us" (Matthew 1:23).

Hebrews 7:26 tells us He was sinless: "Who is holy, harmless, undefiled, separate from sinners." So He was uniquely qualified to cope with sin.

Drinking Problem

Jesus had a drinking problem. We hear of men be-

11

ing driven by life's circumstances to drink. But that only adds problems to problems. Strange as it may seem, Jesus' drinking was part of the solution to the sin problem. What did He drink? and when and where?

The place was the winepress—Gethsemane. The time was just before His crucifixion. But what was in His cup that was such a problem to Him? "O my Father, if it be possible, let this cup pass from me: nevertheless, not as I will, but as thou wilt" (Matthew 26:39).

In that cup was sin and all its fearful consequences. Small wonder it gave Jesus such consternation. Talk about a tiger-by-the-tail! Talk about poison in a cup! There it was. What Jesus did then was to determine once and for all if man could escape sin.

And He drank it—all of it! "For he hath made him to be sin for us, who knew no sin; that we might be made the righteousness of God in him" (2 Corinthians 5:21). "And they crucified him" (Matthew 27:35). "When Jesus therefore had received the vinegar, he said, It is finished: and he bowed his head, and gave up the ghost" (John 19:30).

Then and there sin was finished. The penalty was paid in full. "For in that he died, he died unto sin once [once for all]" (Romans 6:10).

A Turnkey Job

Jesus' death didn't complete the scheme. There was one more item in the package—the Resurrection: "Who was delivered for our offenses, and was raised again for our justification" (Romans 4:25).

And so the gospel (the greatest news ever to reach man) was born. And Paul could write: "Moreover, brethren, I declare unto you the gospel which I preached unto you, which also ye have received, and wherein ye stand. . . . For I delivered unto you first of all that which I also received, how that Christ died for our sins according to the Scriptures; and that he was buried, and that he rose again the third day according to the Scriptures" (1 Corinthians 15:1, 3, 4).

Rejoice! The scheme is complete! It works! Nothing need be added. Nothing dare be deleted.

The Next Move

If Svetlana Alliluyeva had not acted when she did she would still be a prisoner of the Iron Curtain. Her scheme for escape was not enough. She could have thought it up. She could have talked to others about it. She could have written it out in meticulous detail. But without specific action it would have done her no good.

God's scheme for escape is foolproof. It is spelled out clearly in the Bible. It is available to all men. What more can God do?

The next move is ours. The first man got us into our terrible problem by his own choice. The only way out is by our own choice. Now we must act. "But as many as received him, to them gave he power to become the sons of God, even to them that believe on his name" (John 1:12). "He that believeth and is baptized shall be saved; but he that believeth not shall be damned" (Mark 16:16). "Believe on the Lord Jesus Christ, and thou shalt be saved, and thy house" (Acts 16:31).

2

The Big Cover-up

Who can forget Watergate? We may as well try to forget Adam and Eve's fig-leaf aprons. The shock waves of the nation's brashest cover-up left the world stunned and wondering.

But Norman Cousins in an article aptly titled "Watergate on Main Street" carries the problem beyond Watergate. He says: "Whatever response we make to a national scandal, a deeper question will remain. Faced with a steady decline in personal standards, how do we impeach ourselves?" His conclusion is: "Most of all, we need to redevelop the capacity to trust one another and to regain our self-respect."[1]

This is not easy. Cover-up is as old as man, and equally as universal. And as long as a man covers up his misdeeds, he can hardly respect himself or maintain the respect of his fellowman.

Cover-up is unethical and unhealthy, for it tends to be like a smoldering volcanic fire beneath the earth's surface, ever threatening to burst forth with all its devastating fury. Solomon knew this. He wrote about it 700 years before Christ was born: "He that

---

[1]Norman Cousins, "Watergate on Main Street," *Reader's Digest*, August 1974, p. 183.

covereth his sins shall not prosper" (Proverbs 28:13). Add to that an insight from Solzhenitsyn: "In keeping silent about evil, in burying it so deep within us that no sign of it appears on the surface, we are implanting it, and it will rise up a thousandfold in the future."

The problem is, however, that men sense a need to cover up, whether to retain the approval of their fellows or to avoid the consequences of their misdeeds.

Human awareness of the need to cover up springs from an even deeper need of which some are not fully aware. The gut problem is sin. Intuitively man attempts to cover his guilt, but in vain. For "all things are naked and opened unto the eyes of him with whom we have to do" (Hebrews 4:13).

Sane and Guilty

On September 5, 1975, Lynette "Squeaky" Fromme attempted to kill President Gerald Ford. Fortunately she was whisked off to jail and held there until her trial in December.

Before the trial she was carefully examined for mental competency and declared to be sane, and therefore responsible for her own acts. She was subsequently tried, found guilty, and sentenced to life in prison by U. S. District Court Judge Thomas J. MacBride.

For Miss Fromme there was no escape. Justice meted out her just deserts. She was sane and responsible, therefore guilty. And being guilty, she must bear the consequences.

According to the Scripture, man, in his relation to

God, is little different. Like a trial judge, the apostle Paul, writing an opinion by divine inspiration, established the awful guilt of every man: "There is none righteous, no, not one: there is none that understandeth, there is none that seeketh after God. They are all gone out of the way, they are together become unprofitable; there is none that doeth good, no, not one" (Romans 3:10-12).

This leaves man in a terrible state of affairs. He is held responsible: "So then every one of us shall give account of himself to God" (14:12). "And if the righteous scarcely be saved, where shall the ungodly and the sinner appear?" (1 Peter 4:18). He is found guilty: "That every mouth may be stopped, and all the world may become guilty before God" (Romans 3:19). He is under the sentence of death: "The soul that sinneth, it shall die" (Ezekiel 18:20). "For the wages of sin is death" (Romans 6:23). "And sin when it is finished, bringeth forth death" (James 1:15).

Legitimate Cover-up

Is cover-up ever right? Some think ex-President Nixon should have burned his tapes. Others think it is the height of folly to expose the undercover and sometimes questionable activities of the Central Intelligence Agency.

What about the prisoner who turns to Christ? When God has forgiven him is he released from all obligation to society? Need he uncover crimes for which he has not paid?

It is easier to ask questions than to answer them. But one more must be asked: Does God ever pull a cover-up? And, if so, how and why?

The answer is an emphatic "yes." Without doubt, the greatest cover-up in man's history can be credited to God. And besides that, it was all on the "up and up."

In theological terms it is called the "atonement." Atonement is a good Biblical word found 76 times in the Old Testament and once in the New (Romans 5:11). It means covering. The word *atone* means to cover up.

A look at Noah's ark will help us. God told him: "Pitch it within and without with pitch" (Genesis 6:14). An accurate translation could be: "Atone it within and without with an atonement"; or, better yet: "Cover it within and without with a covering."

Atonement usually has to do with sin. That is why the word is so meaningful to us. The big question then is, how can sin be successfully covered? There is no easy way. Those who think so will discover the meaning of "Be sure your sin will find you out" (Numbers 32:23).

In his *Outlines of Theology,* A.A. Hodge provides a valuable insight. He says atonement means "to cover by an expiatory sacrifice."[2] This puts a whole new light on the legitimacy of God's cover-up of sin. Surely God cannot sin, nor can He be party to a scheme that violates the principles of justice. But by His eternal wisdom He conceived the idea of a foolproof cover-up for sin that meets all the requirements of His unimpeachable justice and righteousness.

The word *expiatory* needs closer scrutiny. It is

---

[2]A.A. Hodge, *Outlines of Theology*(Grand Rapids: Zondervan Publishing House, reprinted 1972).

closely akin to the word *expiation,* which means "making reparation for an injury; atoning for a sin; suffering punishment for an offense or crime."

What kind of atonement, then, must be made so God can be just and at the same time be the Justifier of sinful mankind?

Here is the place to say, "Love found the answer." The wise Solomon saw this when he wrote: "Love covereth all sins" (Proverbs 10:12). While he may not have had godly atonement in view, he did perceive the power of true love. Much later Paul sounded the depth of the truth when he announced: "God commendeth his love toward us, in that, while we were yet sinners, Christ died for us" (Romans 5:8). So we conclude that the atonement is love's answer to man's dilemma.

Atonement, in the godly sense, must provide more than a covering to hide, as when a sheet is placed over a dead body. It must provide so absolute a covering as to eliminate the object it conceals. To do this was a costly undertaking, for it necessitated the personal involvement of the Second Person of the Godhead.

Before we pursue an in-depth understanding of Christ's atonement, we need to note the difference between atonement in the two Testaments.

Atonement was very important in the Old Testament, as is indicated by the extensive coverage given to the subject. However, the almost total absence of the term in the New Testament is no indication that the need for atonement was gone, nor that atonement was not accomplished. The exact opposite is true.

Old Testament atonement, while legally acceptable to God and provisionally sufficient for the sinner, was in truth only the shadow of New Testament reality. It could not actually eliminate sin: "For it is not possible that the blood of bulls and of goats should take away sin" (Hebrews 10:4). It did provide a cover-up for sin, which in God's mind was adequate and legitimate. For man's employment of the provision indicated faith, which in turn made it judicially possible for Him to hold off judgment until the true atonement was made.

New Testament atonement, on the other hand, was the perfect cover-up. So adequate and complete was it that when applied it did not only hide sin from view and thus circumvent judgment, but it eliminated sin so completely that it removed the necessity for judgment.

How could this be done? As stated before, love found a way. No mere mortal could have done it. The requirements of divine justice were beyond men and angels. Only a sinless man could qualify. But where to find a sinless man? No ordinary human was fit, for "all have sinned." Nor could an angel qualify, for they are all spirits and have not flesh and blood. "For the life of the flesh is in the blood; and I have given it to you upon the altar to make an atonement for your souls: for it is the blood that maketh an atonement for the soul" (Leviticus 17:11).

The only solution to the problem was to wed God and man, thus making possible a perfectly qualified being who was flesh and blood, and yet sinless in the absolute sense.

Incarnation did it. "And the angel answered and said unto her, The Holy Ghost shall come upon thee, and the power of the Highest shall overshadow thee: therefore also that holy thing which shall be born of

19

thee shall be called the Son of God" (Luke 1:35). "And they shall call his name Immanuel, which being interpreted is, God with us" (Matthew 1:23). "And ye know that he was manifested to take away our sins; and in him is no sin" (1 John 3:5).

However, the appearance of the God-man was not the whole answer. Bethlehem's story is beautiful, but there is no atonement there. Thirty-three years of the God-man moving among men and showing forth God and His ways is most exciting and inspiring. Yet even that could in no way cover up for the evil in man or cure his sin problem. The atonement was not in His *living*.

Not until Calvary was there genuine atonement for sin. It sprang from His *dying!* "Christ died for our sins" (1 Corinthians 15:3). It was the fruit of His shed blood. "Without shedding of blood is no remission" (Hebrews 9:22).

Here is a legitimate cover-up. The cover-up jobs of men are aimed at preservation of the self-life and self-image. The cover-up of Calvary was quite the opposite. It caused our Lord to be "so marred more than any man, and his form more than the sons of men" (Isaiah 52:14), and demanded the laying down of His life.

Watergate was costly. In the end it cost ex-President Nixon the highest office in the land. Yet that cost cannot be compared with the cost of God's cover-up. Atonement is costly. No computer can tally the cost to our Heavenly Father. What price can be placed on an only son? And what of the cost to Jesus? Paul indicates it impoverished Him: "Though he was rich, yet for your sakes he became poor" (2 Corinthians 8:9). There is no poverty like the pov-

20

erty of sin. "For he hath made him to be sin for us" (5:21).

And having been made sin He paid the ultimate penalty—death by crucifixion. What a price! An old adage says: "You get what you pay for." But in the atonement *we* get what *He* paid for.

The Fallout

Fallout is a genuine fear for 20th-century man. He knows the horrors of the A-bomb and H-bomb for he has glimpsed their awful devastation. But he also knows there is something equally as fearful as the initial impact. It is the fallout that follows. For while the bomb may wipe out a city, the fallout may bring slow death and long-lasting destruction to a far greater area.

How different is the fallout from Calvary? It is true the initial impact of that awful day dealt sin the fatal blow. Yet the "shock waves" of that cataclysmic event have carried the "fallout" to men around the world for 20 centuries. And in them is life instead of death; pardon and peace instead of fear and condemnation, healing instead of sickness, riches instead of poverty, glory instead of shame, and restoration instead of destruction. All of this and more is the blessed "fallout" of the atonement.

Life Instead of Death

The Watergate cover-up was the death of Mr. Nixon, at least politically, and maybe in several other ways as well. Most cover-up schemes are like that. They are never quite up to the need. They are like the bed Isaiah describes: "For the bed is shorter than that a man can stretch himself on it: and the covering narrower than that he can wrap himself in it" (Isaiah 28:20). They kill, if not outwardly, at least inwardly. Many a man is dead on the inside because of his cover-up tactics. "He that covereth his sins shall not prosper" (Proverbs 28:13).

But there is more to that verse: "Whoso confesseth and forsaketh them shall have mercy." This is the angle to pursue, for it is the only way to the perfect cover-up.

We can learn a lesson from the grizzly bear. He has enough sense to know his tracks can lead to his destruction, especially at hibernation time. So rather than hibernate on a beautiful calm day, leaving his tracks plainly visible in the snow for a potential destroyer to see, he waits for a fierce storm. Then, making his way to his den, he hasn't a worry. God has wiped out his tracks and he is safe.

In the atonement God provided the perfect "snowstorm" to wipe out the telltale tracks of our sin. All we need to do is avail ourselves of His provision. "If we confess our sins, he is faithful and just to forgive us our sins, and to cleanse us from all unrighteousness" (1 John 1:9). Blessed fallout!

Pardon and Peace Instead of Fear and Condemnation

Fear and condemnation—who can bear them? They are the harvest for sin and its bedfellow, cover-up. They drive men like a taskmaster to sleepless nights; the psychiatrist's couch; drink, drugs, and alcohol; despair; mental hospitals; and suicide.

But why go that route? The atonement makes it unnecessary. (See Colossians 1:20-22.)

Surely the atonement is the perfect cure. The psychoanalyst or the counselor may probe to uncover the cause and he may be successful in searching out some dark corners, but apart from God he cannot effect a perfect cover-up. True, he may help through the therapy of releasing the awful tensions pent up in a bosom. But sin is not cured by being exposed. In the final analysis, atonement is the only answer. It erases the cause for fear and condemnation.

Healing Instead of Sickness

Sin is the most devastating force ever to hit the human race. In its wake comes every known evil—sickness, sorrow, death. While it is a fact that the atonement was aimed primarily at sin, the fallout reached beyond sin to all of its awful consequences.

Sin is universal—so are sickness and death. The atonement encompasses the whole spectrum. Does this mean that man need not experience physical death? Hardly. Although the *ultimate* fallout of the atonement will include even that: "The last enemy that shall be destroyed is death" (1 Corinthians 15:26).

The general order is (1) sin, (2) sickness, and (3) death. The same applies to the atonement. While the atonement encompassed and conquered all three, the experiential outworking of it begins with sin and will finally reach to the farthest perimeter, death.

In the meantime, however, the provision of the atonement is not only adequate to remedy our sicknesses, but God intends that we should, in this life, avail ourselves of that coverage. While covering our sins, the atonement also covers our sicknesses. "Who his own self bare our sins in his own body on the tree, that we, being dead to sins, should live unto righteousness: by whose stripes ye were healed" (1 Peter 2:24).

Riches Instead of Poverty

Sin made all men paupers. Every man was spiritually bankrupt, with no possible human way out. If only a few had been thus bankrupt, others could have come to their rescue. But sin infected all. No man could help his fellow, for all were caught in the same quicksand.

Nevertheless, the atonement covered all of man's bad debts. And not only that—it credited to his account the unlimited treasures of heaven, so that Paul could say: "That ye through his poverty might be rich" (2 Corinthians 8:9).

Glory Instead of Shame

Sin robbed man of glory: "For all have sinned, and come short of the glory of God" (Romans 3:23).

The atonement restored the glory: "And the glory which thou gavest me I have given them" (John 17:22).

Restoration Instead of Destruction

Destruction is the end of sin. "Who shall be punished with everlasting destruction from the presence of the Lord, and from the glory of his power" (2 Thessalonians 1:9).

But destruction was not God's intention anymore than sin was His intention. God gets no pleasure out of it. It is contrary to His nature. "Say unto them, As I live, saith the Lord God, I have no pleasure in the death of the wicked" (Ezekiel 33:11).

In the same verse God bared His great heart when He cried: "But that the wicked turn from his way and live: turn ye, turn ye . . . for why will ye die, O house of Israel?"

The atonement, the great cover-up of the ages, is geared to that glorious end, that all men plunging toward certain destruction might be fully restored and ultimately conformed to the image of His Son.

3

Man, You're Worth a Lot

Did you ever try paying a $400 debt with $75? It's not easy. But Dean Herron did it.

What happened was this. Dean, 11 years old, bought three ponies with money he'd earned scrubbing floors. He boarded the ponies at a farm outside Detroit. Snowmobilers tore down the fence and the ponies ran away.

They were captured just before Christmas by Oakland County Sheriff's officers.

Boarding costs mounted up. Soon they reached $400 and an auction was ordered. The law said they were "animals at large."

Then Dean heard that his ponies were found and ready to be auctioned. All he had was $75. He hoped that would be enough to buy them back.

"Do I hear a bid of $30 for this pony?" Dean was worried. *Thirty dollars for one pony.* . . . "That's too much. You should start at $25," he told them. "Are you bidding?" inquired the auctioneer. "They're my ponies," came the quick reply.

Bidding was delayed a moment for a meeting of minds. The judge, Gerald E. McNally, and the Animal Shelter director, Dr. F. Hugh Wilson, conferred.

26

When bidding began again it was on all three ponies "as a package."

Tom Finley, a friend of the family, placed Dean's bid. It was $75. He had no more. It did the trick. Other would-be bidders heard the story and did not bid. The debt was erased and Dean had his beloved ponies back.

Do you suppose those ponies realized what they were worth to Dean? Of course not. And you and I have no idea what we are worth to God.

What Is Man?

Evidently we are very valuable to God. Why? What does God see in us to get so excited over? Someone else asked that question long ago: "What is man, that thou art mindful of him? and the son of man, that thou visitest him?" (Psalm 8:4).

The Bible has the answer. Some of the world's systems and some of its renowned leaders put a low price tag on a man. For their unrighteous ends millions of humans are expendable. They are simply fodder for their "gristmills." Not so God. He treasures us. And for good reason—He has invested himself in us. "For we are also his offspring" (Acts 17:28).

We are unlike any other earthbound creature. We were not patterned after some other creature, but after God himself. "And God said, Let us make man in our image, after our likeness. . . . So God created man in his own image, in the image of God created he him" (Genesis 1:26, 27).

All of creation bears God's fingerprints, but we alone bear His image. It is this image that makes us

27

so valuable. Investment and interest go together. "For where your treasure is, there will your heart be also" (Matthew 6:21). God invested a great treasure in us.

In the Bible this treasure is called "glory." "Thou crownedst him with glory and honor, and didst set him over the works of thy hands" (Hebrews 2:7). The image and the glory are simultaneous with each other. It's sort of like Siamese twins. Whenever and wherever one is, there is also the other. "But we all . . . are changed into the same image from glory to glory" (2 Corinthians 3:18). "He is the image and glory of God" (1 Corinthians 11:7).

Who can define glory? It's like trying to define God, for glory is the outshining of God. Glory is the outward manifestation of all that is in Him. It is the true riches of heaven. It is the "stuff" with which Jesus was rich before He became poor. "Though he was rich, yet for your sakes he became poor" (2 Corinthians 8:9). He was not rich because He had a bag full of diamonds and gold. But He was rich because He possessed the glory of God. "And now, O Father, glorify thou me with thine own self with the glory which I had with thee before the world was" (John 17:5).

That is the thing that makes us so valuable to God. No other creature on earth has the capacity to partake of His glory. Our worth to God does not accrue from what we can give to God, but from the fact that we are so constituted as to bring the highest pleasure to God by partaking of His glory. "Thou art worthy, O Lord, to receive glory and honor and power: for thou hast created all things, and for thy pleasure they are and were created" (Revelation 4:11).

Lost Treasure

Dean Herron's ponies got lost from their pasture. His big investment brought him no dividends. Instead of pleasure, he had heartache.

God could empathize with him. The fence of His "pasture" got torn down too and his treasured possession went astray. "All we like sheep have gone astray; we have turned every one to his own way" (Isaiah 53:6). "For all have sinned, and come short of the glory of God" (Romans 3:23).

The beautiful purpose for which God made man was interrupted. The glory of God departed. We were empty. The image was unmercifully marred.

The Highest Bidder

To buy at an auction you have to be the highest bidder. Dean Herron knew that. The price a bidder is willing to pay is a fair appraisal of the value he places on the product. Dean was willing to spend all he had.

God's assessment of our value is best understood by the price He paid to buy us back. Dollars can buy back horses but not the souls of men. "Forasmuch as ye know that ye were not redeemed [bought back] with corruptible things, as silver and gold" (1 Peter 1:18).

> God could have given suns of gold, and stars of silver, constellations glowing with precious metals, but none of these would have been sufficient to free one soul from the curse or penalty of sin, or to change it into a loyal and loving subject of His reign.[1]

What price then was God willing to pay for us?

The full price. There was no end-of-the-year sale; no clearance price; no stock-reduction closeout. The price was fixed and firm. There was no bargain counter. The price was the full demand of divine justice. It involved blood and death.

But the blood and death of no ordinary man would satisfy the demands. Old Testament types had made that clear. Rigid requirements applied.

(1) Redemption of a man who was sold required a kinsman-redeemer. "After that he is sold he may be redeemed again; one of his brethren may redeem him: either his uncle, or his uncle's son, may redeem him, or any that is nigh of kin unto him of his family may redeem him; or if he be able, he may redeem himself" (Leviticus 25:48,49).

(2) Redemption which involved forgiveness of sin required the blood sacrifice of a lamb without blemish or spot. "Your lamb shall be without blemish, a male of the first year" (Exodus 12:5).

No angel could fit the bill, for the simple reason that angels are not kin to man. What's more, no man, even though he was of the human race, could qualify to pay the demands of justice. "And he [the Lord] saw that there was no man, and wondered that there was no intercessor" (Isaiah 59:16).

Why couldn't man redeem his fellowman? The fact is, each man has his own problem. First, every man is a sinner and in need of redemption himself: "As it is written, There is none righteous, no, not one" (Romans 3:9). Not a man can be found without some blemish or spot.

---

[1] F. B. Meyer, *Tried by Fire* (Fort Washington, Pennsylvania: Christian Literature Crusade, reprinted 1970).

Second, no man is able to redeem himself or his fellowman. The Law gave him the right if he could. But the price is too high. The man seeking to redeem his fellow would find himself on the horns of a dilemma. For in the process he would have to forfeit his life for his own sin, and then he himself would be dead and certainly unable to pay the price for another. The redemption price for life is life.

Love Found a Way

Who could hurdle the impossible barriers? Who could be both human and sinless? Surely no mortal man; not even the world's greatest leaders or founders of religion. For all were indeed human, but none was sinless.

"Is any thing too hard for the Lord?" (Genesis 18:14). Though the problem was too enormous for any and all of us, God found an answer. Abraham was right when he said, "God will provide himself a lamb" (22:8). The hymnist says, "Love found a way to redeem my soul; love found a way that could make me whole."

Love's way was Jesus: "Ye know that ye were not redeemed with corruptible things, as silver and gold, from your vain conversation received by tradition from your fathers; but with the precious blood of Christ, as of a lamb without blemish and without spot" (1 Peter 1:18, 19).

Jesus met all the demands. He qualified as our kinsman through His incarnation. "Forasmuch then as the children are partakers of flesh and blood, he also himself likewise took part of the same; that through death he might destroy him that had the power of death, that is, the devil. . . . For verily he took not on him the nature of angels; but he took on him the seed of Abraham. Wherefore in all things it behooved him to be made like unto his brethren" (Hebrews 2:14, 16, 17).

He qualified morally. He was the "lamb without blemish and without spot" (1 Peter 1:19). He was without sin: "For we have not a high priest which cannot be touched with the feeling of our infirmities; but was in all points tempted like as we are, yet without sin" (4:15).

The full price was the blood of the spotless Lamb. That was the "sticker price." Nothing less could clench the deal. But why so high a price? It was the only way to clear the title, for it was attached with the "lien" of sin. Paying for sin required death. "Sin, when it is finished, bringeth forth death" (James 1:15).

Why blood? What is the sense of a blood sacrifice? Is God bloodthirsty? Isn't the idea of a blood sacrifice heathenish? The Bible gives the answer: "For the life of the flesh is in the blood; and I have given it to you upon the altar to make an atonement for your souls: for it is the blood that maketh an atonement for the soul" (Leviticus 17:11). To redeem our lives, Jesus had to give His life. Since the life is in the blood, His blood had to be shed. He laid down His life for us.

But rejoice. He was able to take it again. None of us could have done that. "Therefore doth my Father love me, because I lay down my life, that I might take it again. No man taketh it from me, but I lay it down of myself. I have power to lay it down, and I have power to take it again" (John 10:17, 18).

So we see, there was no miscarriage of justice and there was no "under-the-table" deal. The full price was paid. All the demands of justice were met. And the way was clear so God could be "just, and the justifier of him which believeth in Jesus" (Romans 3:26).

Fringe Benefits

Man, you're worth a lot. Think of the price God paid to buy you back. He saw each of us as a treasure in a field. And He bought the whole field to get us back. (See Matthew 13:44.)

But it is not only God who benefits. We also benefit. God has a clear title to us, and we have a clear title to our inheritance in heaven. Think about the fringe benefits we reap:

(1) *We are delivered from the auction block.* The Biblical word *redemption* means to purchase at the slave market, or to set free by paying a price. We were in slavery to Satan and sin. The price on our "heads" was so high none of us could think of paying it. We had sold ourselves with no possible hope of recovery. Then Jesus came. He paid up all accounts owing and none could any longer have a rightful claim on us. We were free! "If the Son therefore shall make you free, ye shall be free indeed" (John 8:36).

(2) *We have the forgiveness of sins.* "In whom we have redemption through his blood, the forgiveness of sins, according to the riches of his grace" (Ephesians 1:7). Let's never get the idea that forgiveness is cheap. Our forgiveness cost Jesus His blood: "The blood of Jesus Christ his Son cleanseth us from all sins. . . . If we confess our sins, he is faithful and just

to forgive us our sins, and to cleanse us from all unrighteousness" (1 John 1:7, 9).

(3) *Our heavenly inheritance is restored.* Sin had a mortgage on it. The ante was far beyond us. There was no way to renew it. We were like Ruth, the lady of Moab. Death had brought her husband's impossible liabilities upon her head. Her inheritance was in jeopardy until Boaz, her kinsman, got into the picture. He valued both Ruth and her inheritance so highly he was willing to pay off the debt, thus freeing Ruth and restoring her inheritance.

Like Ruth, we too were involved in the hopeless mortgage of our inheritance through our father, Adam. But our elder brother, Christ, stepped into the picture. He valued us so highly that He paid off every obligation, setting us free from responsibility and sharing His riches with us.

And on that day, when a multitude that no man can number of all nations, kindreds, people, and tongues shall stand before the throne, clothed with white robes and palms in their hands, they shall sing:

Thou art worthy to take the book, and to open the seals thereof: for thou wast slain, and has redeemed us to God by thy blood out of every kindred, and tongue, and people, and nation; and hast made us unto our God kings and priests: and we shall reign on the earth. And I beheld, and I heard the voice of many angels round about the throne, and the beasts, and the elders: and the number of them was ten thousand times ten thousand, and thousands of thousands; saying with a loud voice, Worthy is the Lamb that was slain to receive power, and riches, and wisdom, and strength, and honor, and glory, and blessing (Revelation 5:9-12).

34

4

Sorry 'bout That

Dr. Harold Manner, Chairman of the Biology Department of Loyola University of Chicago, was a churchgoer through the early years of his life. But college changed all of that. He became an avowed evolutionist and forgot God.

In time he became a recognized authority in his field, and authored several textbooks relating to biological science which are widely circulated today.

Having escaped the church and its "bondage," he was "free" to indulge in the world's pleasures, alcoholism not being the least of them.

But God has His ways. Dr. Manner was lecturing at a conference in a distant city. Returning to his hotel room one night he discovered a Gideon Bible open on his bed. Evidently the maid had been reading it and had inadvertently forgotten to put it back in the drawer. Or was it providential?

Somehow the lines of the open Bible caught Dr. Manner's eye and he began to read. He was fascinated. The more he read the more he wanted to read. By the time he got home he had devoured all four Gospels—and he was hooked.

One thing led to another. The Word generated

desire, and desire led him to a Jimmy Swaggart crusade. Soon he was born again.

But there was a problem—what to do about all those evolutionary textbooks he had written. Now his views were so different.

Could he retract the textbooks? No way. But he could do something. He had had an about-face relating to his past writings, and he could seek to undo the previous damage by writing from his new point of view. This he is doing. He has written another textbook that reflects his current thinking in favor of Creationism.

This is true repentance.

Exposed

On Saturday, February 28, 1976, Norman J. Rees, a retired oil company engineer, was found dead in his retirement village condominium, an apparent suicide.

The F.B.I. identified him as a Soviet informer who turned double agent.

Why had he taken his own life? He was on the verge of being exposed and he couldn't face it.

The *Dallas Times Herald* had dug up the story. They reported Rees admitted giving the Soviet Union valuable information about the U.S. oil and gas industry from 1942 to 1971.

"His delivery to the Soviets of the latest advances in U.S. petroleum technology led one intelligence officer to characterize Rees as the single most important individual in the development of the Russian oil and gas industry during the relevant period (1945-1960)," the *Times Herald* said.

The newspaper reported Rees admitted his connections and that the Soviets had awarded him a medal and a $5000 annual pension for his services.

But Rees couldn't face being exposed. He begged newspaper officials several times not to publish the story and to refrain from identifying him.

Only hours before his suicide he inquired to see if the story would break. The answer was "yes." Unable to face the consequences, he turned his .38-caliber pistol on himself and died before the world learned of his crime.

Being exposed is no easy pill to swallow. There's no candy coating. It's for real and it's a bitter ordeal. Rees feared it. The newspaper was going to tell his story. He could see no way out.

Nobody relishes being exposed. "Men loved darkness rather than light, because their deeds were evil. For every one that doeth evil hateth the light, neither cometh to the light, lest his deeds should be reproved [discovered]" (John 3:19, 20).

But what we don't like is often best for us. Freedom of the press, while it may have its weaknesses, serves a good purpose. For some individuals it serves as a deterrent, and it has a way of purging some of society's evils. It certainly turns the bright lights on men's dark deeds.

All of us need to be exposed. It is good for our souls. It is easy to be on a collision course. We need to be brought to our senses. Remember the shocker Jesus leveled at Peter: "And when thou art converted, strengthen thy brethren" (Luke 22:32)? Who will repent until he knows he's a sinner? Who will get saved until he knows he's lost? Who will alter his course until he glimpses its end?

Hound of Heaven

God has His own way of exposing us. Not that He splashes our evil on the front page for public viewing. But rather, He flashes it on the screen of our conscience for our own viewing. And all the while His goal is in no sense our self-destruction, but our ultimate good. How does He do this?

His principal agent is the Holy Spirit. He is under special assignment to make us aware of our sins: "And when he is come, he will reprove the world of sin, and of righteousness, and of judgment" (John 16:8). He has been reverently dubbed "the Hound of heaven," for it is His objective to search out all men, to make sin exceedingly sinful to them, and to guide them to Jesus.

Ways and Means

Here is how He does it. He uses a man and a Book. The man becomes His mouthpiece and the Book becomes His message. The Holy Spirit works through men who use the sword of the Spirit, the Word of God.

The Bible is full of examples. Jonah is a good one. Nineveh was a city full of wickedness. God said: "Their wickedness is come up before me" (Jonah 1:2). But Nineveh needed to be alerted to its own wickedness which was propelling it rapidly toward doom. Therefore the Lord sent Jonah, saying: "Go to Nineveh, that great city, and cry against it" (v. 2).

Jonah was God's man. God's word was to be the means. His instructions to Jonah were simple and to the point: "Arise, go unto Nineveh, that great city, and preach unto it the preaching that I bid thee" (3:2).

And that preaching was engineered by divine design to expose Nineveh to herself. Unless she could see herself, her fate was fixed. But if she could grasp the depths of her own depravity there would be hope.

John the Baptist was another holy investigator. Like Jonah, he too was commissioned to expose men to themselves and to lay bare their wicked hearts. As always, God uses a man and a message. Surely John had an insight into what God was up to when he cried: "And now also the axe is laid unto the root of the trees: every tree therefore which bringeth not forth good fruit is hewn down, and cast into the fire" (Luke 3:9). When he preached, men saw themselves.

Another Biblical example was Peter. He was God's man, and he had God's message.

There is a subtle temptation to simply pray and then expect God, apart from our participation, to convict the sinner by awakening him to his evil ways. It doesn't work that way. When Jesus was on earth He was full of God's Spirit. "For God giveth not the Spirit by measure unto him" (John 3:34). The Spirit, working freely through Him, caused men to see themselves. Like a mighty X ray, His words exposed the awful cancer of evil: "Woe unto you, scribes and Pharisees, hypocrites! for ye are like unto whited sepulchres, which indeed appear beautiful outward, but are within full of dead men's bones, and of all uncleanness. Even so ye also outwardly appear righteous unto men, but within ye are full of hypocrisy and iniquity" (Matthew 23:27, 28).

Peter, like his Lord, was full of the Holy Ghost.

The Holy Ghost did His "heart analysis" through him. Look at some of his lines: "Him . . . ye have taken, and by wicked hands have crucified and slain" (Acts 2:23). "Therefore let all the house of Israel know assuredly, that God hath made that same Jesus, whom ye have crucified, both Lord and Christ" (v. 36).

The lesson is clear. Men see themselves for what they really are when God's servants, anointed by God's Spirit, fearlessly declare God's Word.

Really Sorry

It's not enough to be exposed or to be found out. Plenty of folks are sorry when this happens, but often they are only sorry that they have been exposed, and not sorry for the sins that have been uncovered.

Modern psychology and psychiatry are confronted with devastating guilt complexes in many lives. People are burdened down with sorrow over past deeds that weigh on their minds day and night. But this kind of sorrow is deadly. Paul told the Corinthians: "The sorrow of the world worketh death" (2 Corinthians 7:10).

The sorrow of the world is toward oneself. It is not sorrow toward God, and there is a vast difference. The sorrow of the world leads toward suicide, as in the case of Judas. Sorrow toward God leads to salvation, as in the case of David.

God's exposure is always aimed at getting us turned around, never at destroying us. God wants to help us, not to hurt us. "Now I rejoice, not that ye were made sorry, but that ye sorrowed to repentance: for ye were made sorry after a godly manner,

40

that ye might receive damage by us in nothing. For godly sorrow worketh repentance to salvation not to be repented of" (vv. 9, 10).

Norman J. Rees was sorry he was caught. He was sorry for himself, but there is no sign he was really sorry toward God for his wrongdoing. So he died.

David was different. He too was exposed. God's prophet did it with a word from the Lord: "And Nathan said to David, Thou art the man. Thus saith the Lord God of Israel . . . wherefore hast thou despised the commandment of the Lord?" (2 Samuel 12:7, 9).

But David did not go out and end it all. Nor did he harden his heart and stoically set his jaw to take the consequences. He was really sorry. Hear his admission: "Against thee, thee only, have I sinned, and done this evil in thy sight" (Psalm 51:4).

When the people of Nineveh saw themselves through Jonah's preaching they too became really sorry. They understood that their evil was so great against God that they were inviting their own destruction. What did they do about it? Did they lightly laugh it off? By no means. They entered into a period of deep and honest sorrow:

> For word came unto the king of Nineveh, and he arose from his throne, and he laid his robe from him, and covered him with sackcloth, and sat in ashes. And he caused it to be proclaimed and published through Nineveh by the decree of the king and his nobles, saying, Let neither man nor beast, herd nor flock, taste any thing: let them not feed, nor drink water: but let man and beast be covered with sackcloth, and cry mightily unto God: yea, let them turn every one from his evil way, and from the violence that is in their hands (Jonah 3:6-8).

41

That was honest-to-goodness repentance. And it saved Nineveh.

The blazing, penetrating preaching of Peter to the crowd in Jerusalem had the same good effect. Instead of running for cover and hiding from the truth, they sought an honest solution. Like an expert prosecuting attorney, Peter, directed by the Spirit, had laid the evidence on the line. At once they were both the tried and the jury. Confronted with such an avalanche of incriminating evidence against themselves, they cried out: "Men and brethren, what shall we do?" (Acts 2:37).

We are reminded of Patty Hearst's trial. One reporter wrote: "The jurors in the trial of Patricia Hearst wanted 'all in our hearts,' as one said, 'to believe that she was innocent,' but they felt obligated to vote for conviction because 'the steady accumulation of evidence against her and the quality of her defense' left them no choice."

On Coming Clean

It is painful and necessary that our sins be uncovered and exposed. It is important that we be truly sorry for our sin. But all of this is not enough. Confession must be added. Confession opens mercy's door.

Confession bares the soul. It removes all the trappings. It is the open and honest admission of guilt. And it is the blessed way to freedom.

Listen to the prodigal son: "I have sinned against heaven, . . . and am no more worthy to be called thy son" (Luke 15:18, 19).

Hear David: "For I will declare my iniquity; I will be sorry for my sin" (Psalm 38:18).

42

Great is god's mercy to the honest confessor. Solomon understood this and wrote: "He that covereth his sins shall not prosper: but whoso confesseth and forsaketh them shall have mercy" (Proverbs 28:13).

An Italian duke boarded a galley ship and questioned the slaves about their offenses. Everyone of them placed the blame on others. One said his brother's crime had brought him there. Another said the judge was unfair. But there was one exception. Upon being questioned he said, "My Lord, I am justly put here. I wanted money and I stole a purse. No one is to blame but myself."

The duke, hearing such an honest confession, seized the man by the shoulder saying, "You rogue! What are you doing among so many 'honest,' 'innocent' men? Get you out of their company."

5

Hands Across the Heavens

A handshake and a Russian bear hug marked the consummation of the Soviet-American union in space in late July 1975.

The two spacecrafts involved in the history-making event were the American Apollo and the Russian Soyuz. "Togetherness in space" someone called it.

Apollo approached Soyuz at the creeping relative speed of one-third of a mile an hour, though both were traveling more than 17,000 miles per hour.

> This orbital togetherness, seen by perhaps a half-billion television viewers around the earth, provided a highly visible demonstration of the real purpose of the flight — detente between the super powers. "When we opened this hatch in space, we were opening back on earth a new era in the history of man," Stafford (one of the American spacemen) declared portentously. "How this new era will go depends on the determination and faith of the peoples of both countries of the world" — *Newsweek,* July 1975.

What a fantastic feat, we say, that could bring two orbiting spacecrafts together, enabling them to link up so they could fly as one craft. We can hardly comprehend the genius and scientific technology that made it happen. We call it a modern miracle. But I know an even greater miracle, the faith that brings together a hopeless sinner and the holy God. There is no togetherness like it.

As we have noted, God has already made available a super plan of salvation that is adequate to save all men. But the plan itself can save no one, anymore than an architect's drawings can build a house. The plan has to be applied. And faith does it: "For by grace are ye saved through faith" (Ephesians 2:8). Faith is at the very basis of repentance and conversion. It is the only force to unite man's need with God's provision, and thus effect true detente between alienated man and his Maker.

Only One Way

We are ingenious at devising ways and means, but we have a big problem. Something in us cries out for union with God: "As the hart panteth after the water brooks, so panteth my soul after thee, O God" (Psalm 42:1). So we go about devising a way to God. By now there must be thousands of them.

Almost every religion on earth has its "way to God," and even the nonreligious have theirs. From earliest man up to man at the end of the 20th century, the list has steadily grown. And when these many "ways" are examined it will be discovered that in every case faith is the essential element. But the fruit of faith is only as good as the foundation upon which it stands.

Adam's firstborn son, Cain, placed his faith in his own reason and offered a bloodless sacrifice, only to discover his "way" didn't work. "But unto Cain and to his offering he [God] had not respect" (Genesis 4:5).

Modern youth place their faith in an equally fruitless "way." Floyd McClung Jr., who has had marked success ministering to young people on the hippie trail describes the "way" of the counterculture:

> I had seen kids by the scores who were turning off their minds, singing the Eastern chants, trying to submit themselves to some vaguely anticipated religious experience. They craved a mystical event of some kind, any kind, with pathetic sincerity. They followed the gurus in chanting their auummmm — their desperation for a piece of God unmistakably real.[1]

Through the fleeting centuries, men have placed their faith in all kinds of "ways," all the way from great personalities and self-styled messiahs to their own good works, their brand of religion, and even to the reasonings of their own minds. But their faith has led them down a dead-end street. For "there is a way which seemeth right unto a man; but the end thereof are the ways of death" (Proverbs 14:12).

There is only one way—the way of faith in God, His Word, and His Son. Faith in anyone or anything less will never effect God's salvation in our lives.

The Bible is positive about this. Jesus said: "Ye believe in God, believe also in me" (John 14:1). Again He said: "He that believeth and is baptized shall be saved" (Mark 16:16). And listen to Paul's admonition to Timothy: "And that from a child thou hast known the holy Scriptures, which are able to

---

[1]Floyd McClung Jr., *Just Off Chicken Street* (Old Tappan, N.J.: Fleming H. Revell, 1975).

46

make thee wise unto salvation through faith which is in Christ Jesus" (2 Timothy 3:15). Add to that the ringing answer the Philippian jailor got when he cried: "Sirs, what must I do to be saved? And they said, Believe on the Lord Jesus Christ, and thou shalt be saved, and thy house" (Acts 16:30, 31).

Dissecting Faith

Dissection is a necessary part of premed experience. Through it the student becomes acquainted with what's beneath the surface of the body. This knowledge then hopefully prepares him for dealing with physical problems in the future.

Too often faith, like the human body, is misunderstood. But since it is so vital to spiritual life, even as the inner workings of the body are vital to natural life, some in-depth probing is necessary.

A. W. Tozer expressed his concern about this:

> Because faith is so vital to all our hopes, so necessary to the fulfillment of every aspiration of our hearts, we dare take nothing for granted concerning it. Anything that carries with it so much of weal or woe, which indeed decides our heaven or our hell, is too important to neglect. We simply must not allow ourselves to be uninformed or misinformed. We must know.
>
> For a number of years my heart has been troubled over the doctrine of faith as it is received and taught among evangelical Christians everywhere. Great emphasis is laid upon faith in orthodox circles, and that is good; but still I am troubled. Specifically, my fear is that the modern conception of faith is not the Biblical one;

[2]A. W. Tozer, *Man, the Dwelling Place of God* (Harrisburg, PA: Christian Publications, Inc.), p. 30.

that when the teachers of our day use the word they do not mean what Bible writers meant when they used it.

Plain horse sense ought to tell us that anything that makes no change in the man who professes it makes no difference to God either.[2]

What then is this particular kind of faith that saves the soul and brings the alienated man into vital union with his Creator?

(1) It is total dependence on God and His Son, Jesus Christ.

(2) It is the soul responding to the Biblically revealed divine character.

(3) It is God's gift to the repentant soul, having nothing to do with the senses or the input they provide.

(4) It is a miraculous ability, given by God, to trust the Son.

(5) It is in its very essence, moral—that is, it is essentially linked to obedience.

"Just Believe God!"

How often we have heard that line, as if believing God is like flying to Mars by some simple mental maneuver. Often the unwitting victim of such senseless advice strains every fiber to obey the order, only to find himself in about the same predicament as the man who attempts to fly by waving a few feathers.

One thing we must get straight—faith is dependent on knowledge. Knowing is as important to believing as the foundation is to a skyscraper. "How then shall they call on him in whom they have not believed? and how shall they believe in him of whom they have not heard? . . . So then faith cometh

48

by hearing, and hearing by the word of God" (Romans 10:14, 17).

The Law of Faith

There is a discernible law of faith in the Bible. It has three simple steps: (1) the word of faith, (2) the work of faith, and (3) the wonder of faith.

This law is absolute. The sequence of the steps is unalterable. The law is at once amazingly simple and utterly profound.

The starting point is the *word of faith*. There's no use attempting the work of faith without it. It cannot be done. The Romans got it from Paul's pen: "The word is nigh thee, even in thy mouth, and in thy heart: that is, the word of faith, which we preach" (v. 8).

The word of faith is the knowledge which is faith's raw material. Even the Gentile centurion of Matthew 8 perceived the principle. He understood that if he had just a word of faith from Jesus, he could expect healing for his sick servant. So he pleaded: "Speak the word only, and my servant shall be healed" (v. 8).

But the word of faith, by itself, is not enough. It must be followed by the *work of faith*. The *word* brings knowledge. The *work* brings action. Apart from action, faith—Biblical faith—cannot exist.

Combine the word of faith with the work of faith and the inevitable result is the *wonder of faith*. In Matthew 28:19, 20 is the record of Jesus' *word of faith* to His disciples: "Go ye therefore, and teach all nations, baptizing them in the name of the Father, and of the Son, and of the Holy Ghost: teaching them

49

to observe all things whatsoever I have commanded you: and, lo, I am with you alway, even unto the end of the world." Through this word of faith came knowledge regarding both the will of God for their future ministry and the presence of God with them to the end of the age.

Then came the *work of faith*. "And they went forth, and preached every where . . ." (Mark 16:20). The word of faith would have been as fruitless as the barren fig tree had the disciples not done the work of faith.

When the work of faith, precipitated by the word of faith, is done, the *wonder of faith* is as natural as day following night: "The Lord working with them, and confirming the word with signs following" (v. 20).

How to Do It

There are two sides to faith, the Godward and the manward. The Bible tells us: "God hath dealt to every man the measure of faith" (Romans 12:3). Furthermore, Jesus is called "the author and finisher of our faith" (Hebrews 12:2).

Really, the whole Godhead is involved in producing faith in us. At the same time, we must realize this is never done apart from us. That is to say, God does not arbitrarily give faith to some and not to others. He gives to all who will have it; to all who respond to the Holy Spirit.

On the manward side there is the hearing and the doing. God gives the Word, but man must hear and respond. Peter's insight will help us here: "Seeing ye have purified your souls in obeying the truth through the Spirit . . . being born again, not of corruptible seed, but of incorruptible, by the word of God, which liveth and abideth for ever" (1 Peter 1:22, 23).

On Buying Without Money

Faith is heaven's medium of exchange. It reaches across the heavens, joining God's limitless supply with our overwhelming need. "Come ye, buy, and eat; yea, come, buy wine and milk without money and without price" (Isaiah 55:1).

The really important things are obtained only by faith. Not just faith in faith, but faith in God and in His eternal Word.

(1) *Eternal life:* "He that heareth my word, and believeth on him that sent me, hath everlasting life, and . . . is passed from death unto life" (John 5:24).

(2) *Forgiveness of sin:* "Since we heard of your faith in Christ Jesus, . . . in whom we have redemption through his blood, even the forgiveness of sins" (Colossians 1:4, 14).

(3) *Righteousness:* "Not having mine own righteousness, which is of the law, but that which is through the faith of Christ, the righteousness which is of God by faith" (Philippians 3:9).

(4) *Joy:* ". . . Believing, ye rejoice with joy unspeakable and full of glory" (1 Peter 1:8).

(5) *Peace:* "Now the God of hope fill you with all joy and peace in believing, that ye may abound in hope, through the power of the Holy Ghost" (Romans 15:13).

6

Eenie-meenie-minie-mo

Life is stranger than fiction. When I was a beginner preacher several decades ago, I was attending a district council session. Discussions of business issues were mingled with elections. We were ready to vote for assistant district superintendent and the man I wanted in office had the same initials as mine, R. L.

At the same time the discussion on the floor interested me greatly. In fact, I was so completely absorbed in it that I was giving little thought to the election.

Ballots were passed. I quickly wrote on mine and turned my attention again to the discussion which was in full swing.

The tellers were picking up the ballots when my wife said to me, "You aren't going to vote for him, are you?" "Why not?" I asked. "Look at your ballot," she whispered. I looked and to my astonishment read, R. L. *Brandt!*

If my wife had not observed my ballot, I would have wondered, when the tellers reported, who had foolishly voted for a novice like me.

We can be very sure God does not foolishly or arbitrarily select any for salvation. He does not play games. He does not have some childish "eenie-meenie-minie-mo" system for determining who will be saved and who will be lost. We can assure our hearts also that God is completely righteous in His determination of who will be saved and who will be lost: "Shall not the Judge of all the earth do right?" (Genesis 18:25).

Nevertheless, the Biblical doctrine of election has been the focal point of much controversy and many questions through the centuries. Here are a few of the questions that continually surface: (1) Are men elected to salvation? (2) Are some elected to damnation? (3) Does God predestinate some to be saved and others to be lost? (4) Does God in His sovereignty reckon at all with the will of man?

Election, in the Biblical sense, means something quite different from the daily usage of the word. G. Raymond Carlson observes:

> When we speak of an election, we are referring to candidates running for an office. The decision is made by the people who vote for them or against them. If the majority cast their votes for one candidate, he is elected; if the majority vote against him, he is not elected. In the Bible the word *election* implies choice also, but it is in an entirely different sense from the ordinary use of the word.[1]

In theological circles there are two quite distinct schools of thought—Calvinism and Arminianism. John Calvin, the founder of Calvinism, strongly emphasized the sovereignty of God, holding to the be-

---

[1]G. Raymond Carlson, *Salvation* (Springfield, MO: Gospel Publishing House, 1963), p. 39.

lief of unconditional predestination. Arminius, the father of Arminianism, held the concept of the freedom of the human will.

Schaff, a church historian of repute, observed:

> Calvinism emphasizes divine sovereignty and free grace; Arminianism emphasizes human responsibility. The one restricts the saving grace to the elect; the other extends it to all men on the condition of faith. Both are right in what they assert; both are wrong in what they deny. If one important truth is pressed to the exclusion of another truth of equal importance, it becomes error, and loses its hold upon the conscience.

Related to the word *election,* and bearing heavily on its true meaning, are two additional Biblical terms —*foreknowledge* and *predestination.* The separation of one of these words from the others, and the consideration of each of them alone and apart from the others, leads toward an unbalanced view, and sometimes to cruel and vicious doctrines.

Formula for Election

Free will plus foreknowledge plus predestination equals election. Election is not solely dependent on sovereign predestination apart from human will. Otherwise, much of the Bible would be meaningless, for it is replete with appeals to the will of man; as for example, Revelation 22:17: "And whosoever will, let him take the water of life freely."

Freedom of the will is inherent to our nature. It is a reflection of the image of God, in whose image we were made.

God will never for any reason violate the principle of free moral agency. As A. W. Tozer says: "For God to override man's freedom and force him to act contrary to his own will would be to make a mockery of the image of God in man."

Tennyson perceived this freedom of the will when he wrote:

> *Thou seemest human and divine,*
> *The highest, holiest manhood, Thou;*
> *Our wills are ours, we know not how;*
> *Our wills are ours, to make them thine.*

The Biblical account of the rich young ruler illustrates the principle. Looking upon the young man as he departed, Jesus made no attempt to coerce or follow him. He had made his choice. It must not be changed by another. And he must bear the consequences of that choice, though it lead him to eternal damnation. For the moral universe, this is better than his being forced into a heaven which he did not choose.

So election is related to the will of the elected. J. Elwin Orr tells of the black preacher who observed, "I never yet knowed nobody elected that wasn't a candidate."

The doctrines of unconditional election and irresistible grace, which simply mean that salvation comes by God's willing it, spawn yet another doctrine known as limited atonement. Limited atonement means that Christ's sacrificial death was for only the elect. But this view seems to go beyond Biblical revelation and is indeed in conflict with it. For Paul wrote: "Your Master also is in heaven; neither is there respect of persons with him" (Ephesians 6:9).

God does not will for some to be saved and for others to be lost. "The Lord . . . is long-suffering to us-ward, not willing that any should perish, but that all should come to repentance" (2 Peter 3:9). "God our Saviour; who will have all men to be saved, and to come unto the knowledge of the truth" (1 Timothy 2:3, 4).

To this end He provided an atonement for *all*. "And he is the propitiation for our sins: and not for ours only, but also for the sins of the whole world" (1 John 2:2).

The order then is: (1) God's provision, (2) man's choice, and (3) God's election. But this presents a theological problem, for from the Biblical point of view it appears election precedes man's choice. Perhaps this brings into focus the heart of the problem. We are such creatures of time we cannot escape its bondage, even in our theology. But God is above time. Time is but a tool for the execution of His plan.

From our vantage point we tend to consider such terms as *predestinate* and *election* in relation to a time-oriented concept, with the result that we force upon the Scriptures what they do not really intend. And we join the saintly old predestinarian in her ridiculous conclusion that "What is to be, will be if it never happens!"

In God's mind Jesus was slain before the world was ever founded. Also in His mind the knowledge of our individual decisions was as real to Him before we ever actually existed as it is after we have actually made them. This then brings us to the key to the whole problem—foreknowledge. If we who are so time-oriented can encompass, at least to a degree, the concept of God's foreknowledge, we can then also in a measure escape the bondage time tends to impose on our theology.

Therefore, predestination and election must not be left standing alone. They must be tied to foreknowledge. "For whom he did foreknow, he also did predestinate" (Romans 8:29). "Elect according to the foreknowledge of God the Father" (1 Peter 1:2).

"Thus," according to *Pulpit Commentary*, "election has its origin in the foreknowledge of the Father; it is wrought out in the sanctifying influences of the Spirit as its sphere and, it issues in active obedience. Obedience is the sign and test of God's election. 'By their fruits ye shall know them.' The end of election is obedience first, then everlasting life."[2]

Vote for Yourself

Is it all right to vote for yourself? We have heard of candidates for certain church offices who received every vote. For whom does a candidate for United States president vote?

We won't try to decide here whether voting for one's self for church or political office is right or wrong. But one thing is certain. Anyone who wants to be elected by God must "vote" for himself. He must do the choosing. What truth in Scripture is set forth more forcefully?

While God makes every righteous and reasonable effort to bring us to himself, He leaves the decision

---

[2]H. D. Spence and T. S. Excell, eds., *Pulpit Commentary* (Grand Rapids: Wm. B. Eerdmans Publishing Co., reprinted 1959).

strictly with us. Apart from our willing, God's hands are tied. "And ye will not come to me, that ye might have life" (John 5:40). "How often would I have gathered thy children together, as a hen doth gather her brood under her wings, and ye would not!" (Luke 13:34).

The appeal of God calls clearly for action on our part. "Behold, I stand at the door, and knock: if any man hear my voice, and open the door, I will come in to him, and will sup with him, and he with me" (Revelation 3:20).

Were there not human responsibility, preaching would be folly. The gospel is God's appeal to man for decision and action. "Go ye into all the world, and preach the gospel to every creature. He that believeth and is baptized shall be saved; but he that believeth not shall be damned" (Mark 16:15, 16). "For God so loved the world, that he gave his only begotten Son, that whosoever believeth in him should not perish, but have everlasting life" (John 3:16). "Sirs, what must I do to be saved? . . . Believe on the Lord Jesus Christ, and thou shalt be saved" (Acts 16:30, 31).

How to Guarantee Your Election

Candidates for political office wish they could find a surefire method for getting elected. They gather around themselves able and influential people; they seek strong financial support so they can properly promote and advertise; and they travel, make speeches, and kiss babies. Yet they are seldom sure of election until the electorate acts.

Peter tells us this need not be so for us: "Wherefore the rather, brethren, give diligence to make your calling and election sure: for if ye do these things, ye shall never fall" (2 Peter 1:10).

"These things" is a clear reference to what has gone before, and indicates we can do something about guaranteeing our own election. We are not to be the victims of whims and notions of men, nor are we at the mercy of an unreasonable God who casts lots to determine our fate. But we are in the driver's seat with all the advantages a loving and concerned God can heap upon us to help us win.

Here is what we must do to guarantee our election:

(1) The starting point is faith, whereby we become partakers of the divine nature, and whereby also we escape the corruption that is in the world through lust. (See 2 Peter 1:4.) But we must understand that this is only the starting point. Election is not guaranteed merely on the basis of entering the race. It is how we run that counts. "Ye did run well; who did hinder you that ye should not obey the truth?" (Galatians 5:7). "Let not him that girdeth on his harness boast himself as he that putteth it off" (1 Kings 20:11).

(2) According to Peter, election is guaranteed on the basis of addition. In mathematics, addition can be done even if we begin with a zero. (For example: $0+1=1$; $0+10=10$.) But this is not true in spiritual life, at least in the sense of advantage. Before "these things" can be added, there must be faith. Nothing plus virtue equals nothing to aid us in making our election sure. But faith plus virtue equals great advantage.

"Add to your faith virtue" (2 Peter 1:5). Virtue is Christian manliness and active courage in the good

59

fight of faith. There is no room for cowardice, mediocrity, or shabbiness, and no room for the soft. For the "Demases" there is no assurance of election. (See 2 Timothy 4:10.)

(3) "Add . . . to virtue, knowledge" (2 Peter 1:5). Not just any old kind of knowledge will do. It is knowledge of a particular sort that Peter envisions — the knowledge of God. Ordinary secular, scientific knowledge can inflate a man's ego and undermine his election, but the knowledge of God helps tighten the cinch. The prophet voiced it well when he cried: "My people are destroyed for lack of knowledge" (Hosea 4:6). Knowledge has a direct bearing on faith, for faith can seldom, if ever, transcend knowledge. So add knowledge.

(4) Add "temperance" (2 Peter 1:6). Temperance is self-control. It is proper balance in legitimate things, and encompasses a broad spectrum, including physical appetites (Proverbs 23:2), sex (Hebrews 13:4), sleep (Proverbs 6:9-11), speech (Colossians 4:6; Titus 2:8; Ephesians 5:4), and the control of our spirits (Proverbs 14:29; 16:32; 25:28). While intemperance tends to erode assurance of election, temperance in all things is another article in the guarantee.

(5) Add "patience" (2 Peter 1:6). Patience is cheerful endurance, constancy. From whence do we get it? By simply permitting tribulation to do its work: "Tribulation worketh patience" (Romans 5:3); and by the Holy Ghost: "Strengthened with all might, according to his glorious power, unto all patience and long-suffering with joyfulness" (Colossians 1:11).

(6) Add "godliness" (2 Peter 1:6). Godliness is

piety. Piety is reverence for God and duty toward Him. Godliness is both friendship with God and willing servitude toward God. It must be in bold print on the conditions of the guarantee.

(7) Add "brotherly kindness" (2 Peter 1:7). Kindness will get you somewhere! It flows out of the grace of God, if given half a chance. It is shown to us through Jesus. "That in the ages to come he might show the exceeding riches of his grace, in his kindness toward us, through Christ Jesus" (Ephesians 2:7).

The same kindness is to flow toward our brothers through us—in consideration of their feelings, in unwillingness to wound or hurt, and in tender concern. By giving this kindness we get it for ourselves.

(8) Add "charity" (2 Peter 1:7). Charity is love. It is named last, but it is not least. Actually it is the capstone of all the virtues. One might have some of the virtues without love, but he cannot have love without having the other virtues. The other virtues are like the sections of an orange, while love is the whole orange.

Nowhere does the Bible say, "God is virtue, knowledge, temperance, patience, godliness, or brotherly kindness." But it does say, "God is love." To have love is to have God. To have God is to have His virtues. To have all of "these things" is to make our calling and election sure and to guarantee for ourselves that we will never fall and we will have an entrance "abundantly into the everlasting kingdom of our Lord and Saviour Jesus Christ" (2 Peter 1:11). There is no "eenie-meenie-minie-mo" about it!

7

This Recycling Business

These days we are recycling just about everything — old car bodies, aluminum cans, weathered boards, used oil, and even garbage.

Recycling takes the old and makes it new. It takes the worn and useless, making it beautiful and useful again.

But do you know God was in the recycling business long before man ever thought of the idea?

We conceive of the original product being perfect. All of creation, according to God's own Word was "very good" (Genesis 1:31).

What about man? Evolutionists think of original man, or more accurately man in his earliest stages, as a wiggling pollywog or even some lesser form of life. But faith in the God of the Bible can hardly allow or espouse such a view.

There is good reason to believe that the great Creator, who is himself the epitome of perfection, made a perfect specimen when He made man in His own image and after His own likeness. For the object is but a reflection of its creator.

The Bible and the evolutionist hold vastly different views on the original state. The hard-core evolutionist believes that the first "life," a primordial "ooze," evolved over eons of time into all of the forms of animal, plant, and human life we know today. He conceives of man as moving from the infantile and insignificant form to an ever higher form until he is virtually a god.

But the Bible supports a vastly different view. It reveals man at the point of origin in the image of God, perfect in every way—physically, mentally, and spiritually, but descending from that lofty estate until he worships the creature rather than his Creator:

> Because that, when they knew God, they glorified him not as God, neither were thankful; but became vain in their imaginations, and their foolish heart was darkened. Professing themselves to be wise, they became fools, and changed the glory of the uncorruptible God into an image made like to corruptible man, and to birds, and four-footed beasts, and creeping things (Romans 1:21-23).

In this state we are useless and hopeless and ready for burning. But God has higher plans for man than this, and that's why He is in the recycling business.

A First in Recycling

The whole Bible bears witness to Satan's destructive nature. His everlasting bent is toward destruction. Look at what happened to Job when the hedge was down and Satan was at liberty to do his thing. Job's oxen and asses were stolen, his servants were slain, his sheep and other servants were consumed with fire, his camels were also stolen, his sons and daughters were killed by a great wind, and his own health was taken away. (See Job 1; 2.)

63

Satan is a habitual criminal. Jesus' description of him in John 10:10 summarizes his unchangeable life-style: "The thief cometh not, but for to steal and to kill, and to destroy."

His destructive work began before man was ever created. There is good reason to believe that when God created the earth, it was perfect. Yet the Genesis record has hardly begun when we are confronted with a description of its condition which is hardly compatible with His revealed nature: "And the earth was without form, and void; and darkness was upon the face of the deep" (Genesis 1:2).

Chaos and darkness belie Satan. Chaos is the inevitable fruit of his doing and darkness is almost synonymous with his name. His power is called "the power of darkness" (Luke 22:53). His deeds are called "the works of darkness" (Romans 13:12). His realm is called darkness: ". . . called you out of darkness" (1 Peter 2:9).

Therefore it is not unreasonable to think the chaotic earth with its prevailing darkness was the fruit of satanic activity. In this state it was meaningless and useless. That's when recycling began: "And the Spirit of God moved upon the face of the waters. And God said, Let there be light: and there was light" (Genesis 1:2, 3).

Resulting from this process was a regenerated earth fitted to God's purpose for an arena in which would be carried out the great drama of humanity.

On the Junk Heap

There is an evident progression relating to the earth in Genesis: (1) perfect creation, (2) satanic intrusion, (3) a "without form and void" state, (4) divine intervention, and (5) regeneration.

A similar progression is to be found relating to man. Man had a fantastic beginning. He was made by God and for God: "For thou hast created all things, and for thy pleasure they are and were created" (Revelation 4:11). He was clothed with God's glory and endowed with the highest mental and physical qualities. So great was his mental acumen that he was able to give names to all other living creatures: "And Adam gave names to all cattle, and to the fowl of the air, and to every beast of the field" (Genesis 2:20). And so excellent was his physical condition that even though the death principle was activated by sin's entry, he lived to be nearly 1000 years old: "And Adam lived an hundred and thirty years, and begat . . . Seth: and the days of Adam after he had begotten Seth were eight hundred years" (Genesis 5:3, 4).

But God's masterpiece of creation didn't last long. Necessary to God's high purpose for man was his endowment with free moral agency. This made man master of his own destiny, but it also made him vulnerable to satanic forces which were bent on his destruction. Adam and Eve soon discovered they were no match for them — but too late. Like the earth itself, they were all but destroyed. No longer could they enjoy blessed communion with their Creator, nor could they fulfill His glorious purpose.

Like a wrecked car, they were ready for the junk heap. The original beauty was gone. The image of the Creator was hardly visible. Their light had turned into darkness. "If therefore the light that is in thee be darkness, how great is that darkness!" (Matthew 6:23).

Total Loss

The Appraiser wrote them and their offspring off as a total loss. Here is His brief:

> There is none righteous, no, not one: there is none that understandeth, there is none that seeketh after God. They are all gone out of the way, they are together become unprofitable; there is none that doeth good, no, not one. Their throat is an open sepulcher; with their tongues they have used deceit; the poison of asps is under their lips: whose mouth is full of cursing and bitterness: their feet are swift to shed blood: destruction and misery are in their ways: and the way of peace have they not known: there is no fear of God before their eyes (Romans 3:10-18).

Is there any hope in the midst of such hopelessness? Can any good thing come from such a sorry state of affairs? What hope is there for any of us, since we all fall into the same category? "Can the Ethiopian change his skin, or the leopard his spots?" (Jeremiah 13:23). "Can he [a man] enter the second time into his mother's womb, and be born?" (John 3:4).

A Ray of Hope

Apart from God there is no hope. But let's learn a lesson from the earth. When it lay in utter chaos and ruin, God, by His Spirit, recycled it and made it beautiful and useful again. What He did for earth He can do for man.

A visit to a potter's house could be an eye-opener

too. "Then I went down to the potter's house, and, behold, he wrought a work on the wheels. And the vessel that he made of clay was marred in the hand of the potter: so he made it again another vessel, as seemed good to the potter" (Jeremiah 18:3, 4).

How Can a Man Be Recycled?

Nicodemus got the answer directly from the Lord: "Ye must be born again" (John 3:7).

The logical question is, "How?" That's what Nicodemus wondered when Jesus confronted him with: "Except a man be born again, he cannot see the kingdom of God" (v. 3). Remember his response: "How can a man be born when he is old?" (v. 4).

And Jesus explained: "Except a man be born of water and of the Spirit, he cannot enter into the kingdom of God" (v.5). But the explanation needs an explanation. What does it mean to be born of water and of the Spirit?

Some teach that water is a reference to baptism, and they arrive at a doctrine known as baptismal regeneration. They believe that God recycles us through the act of baptism.

Others hold that water is a reference to the "water of the word." To support their view they cite Ephesians 5:26: "That he might sanctify and cleanse it with the washing of water by the word."

But Jesus had neither view in mind. He was simply talking of two births and differentiating between them, which Nicodemus was unable to do. The first birth was the natural. Nicodemus thought the second must be like the first, but Jesus made it clear the

67

second was to be different from the first. The first was natural, the second spiritual. The first was "of water," the second was "of the Spirit." "That which is born of the flesh is flesh; and that which is born of the Spirit is spirit" (John 3:6).

How then can we be born spiritually? Natural birth is the fruit of corruptible seed. Without a seed, birth is a positive impossibility. Spiritual birth too is dependent on planted seed. "Being born again, not of corruptible seed, but of incorruptible, by the word of God, which liveth and abideth for ever" (1 Peter 1:23).

Paul had this in mind when he wrote to the Corinthians: "For in Christ Jesus I have begotten you through the gospel" (1 Corinthians 4:15). In his thinking, the gospel was the good seed of the Kingdom, which resulted in the spiritual rebirth of the Corinthians.

The heart of man is like the womb wherein conception takes place. Therein must be the determination of birth. John states it thus: "But as many as received him, to them gave he power to become the sons of God, even to them that believe on his name: which were born, not of blood, nor of the will of the flesh, nor of the will of man, but of God" (John 1:12, 13).

When the good seed of the Word, quickened by the Holy Spirit, finds response and acceptance in the human heart, the glorious result is new birth. That is the ultimate recycling process. It makes the sinner into a saint. It takes that which is fit only for hell and makes it fit for heaven. It takes that which is mortal and corruptible and makes it immortal and incorruptible.

A Brand-new Man

There is a mystery about God's recycling process. We cannot reason it out. With Nicodemus, we are prone to ask: "How can these things be?" (John 3:9). But it is a good idea to remember Jesus' admonition: "Marvel not . . . " (v. 7). The idea is, don't wonder or try to figure it out, for it is as mysterious as the invisible, incomprehensible wind. Only know it works.

Benito Mussolini once observed: "There is no revolution which can change human nature. If such a thing existed, it would be the only revolution worthy of the name, because it would reach down to the primary forces and acquisitive instincts which dominate human activities, and would change them." Evidently he did not know of God's recycling process—the new birth—for the new birth does change the primary forces and acquisitive instincts that dominate human activities.

In fact, God's recycling process produces a brand-new man: "If any man be in Christ, he is a new creature [creation]: old things are passed away; behold, all things are become new" (2 Corinthians 5:17).

Writing of the "fallout" from the revolutionizing new-birth experience, G. Raymond Carlson says:[1]

The greatest effect of experiencing the new birth is that there is a complete change. Our natures change because we become "partakers of the divine nature" (2 Peter 1:4). Our destinies change because fellowship with God is restored. We "have put on the new man,

---

[1] G. Raymond Carlson, *Salvation*, p. 52.

which is renewed in knowledge after the image of him that created him" (Colossians 3:10).

There is a change of direction, not only of life as lived in the present, but also of eternal destiny. There is a change of perspective—old things pass away and everything becomes new. A converted person looks beyond the things which are seen and which are transitory to the things which are not seen and which are eternal. Our desires change because we see this world as God sees it, and we evaluate matters with something of God's perspective. We live an overcoming life. "For whatsoever is born of God overcometh the world: and this is the victory that overcometh the world, even our faith" (1 John 5:4).

Our attitudes change because we have the love of God in our hearts. This brings a change in the objects of our love. Before, we loved ourselves; now we love God and our fellowmen. Before, we loved this present world (1 John 2:15); now we love those things which will never perish for they are eternal. Overflowing and outgoing love replaces selfish desires. "We know that we have passed from death unto life, because we love the brethren. He that loveth not his brother abideth in death" (1 John 3:14).

8

When You Know You Know

It's nice to know who you are.

Maxine Williams tells how she used to worry when she was a small girl that she was not really a Williams by birth. She got the notion somehow that she was taken into the family and that the whole thing was kept a secret. You can imagine her distress over the idea.

But her concern was simply the fruit of her childish and fertile imagination. It had no foundation in fact, for she was indeed born into the Williams family.

As she grew older she was able to escape her frustrating notion. She found all the evidence she needed. She had the sure word of her trustworthy parents. She had a valid birth certificate. And besides that, all she had to do was look at herself in a mirror, for her features were unmistakably Williams'.

Some Christians have a similar problem finding assurance that they are really God's children. They worry and fret and look for some feeling. And often, the more they pursue it, the less they have it.

What's the solution to this problem? Is there some sound approach to genuine assurance and peace of mind? Can a Christian really know he is a child of God?

Assurance Is Based on Evidence

There are two basic kinds of evidence—*external* and *internal*. Both are important to Christian assurance, for one is the fruit of the other. This is the precise point where difficulty often arises.

We tend to look inwardly for assurance. We look for some feeling or some inward token, while at the same time we neglect the basis from which the inward assurance springs.

Feelings, by themselves, can be very fickle. They can be affected by physical well-being or lack of it, by cyclic lows and highs which even the best athletes experience, by good or bad news, and by a host of other influences.

We'd all be smart to heed Luther's insight on this:

For feelings come, and feelings go,
And feelings are deceiving;
My warrant is the Word of God,
Naught else is worth believing.

Documentary Evidence

Our greatest ground for assurance is the Bible itself. All stands or falls on the credibility of this document.

The Bible has survived every test—the test of time, the test of atheistic attempts to destroy it, the test of higher criticism, the test of mockery and subtle denial of its divine inspiration.

What really counts then is what the Bible says.

Having acted in its light and having accepted Jesus as our personal Saviour, we have a sure word on which to base our assurance.

> To those who have thus come to Christ for salvation there can be no other conclusion, if Christ's word is honored, than that they have been received and saved. The Word of God thus becomes a title deed to eternal life, and it should be treated as an article of surety, for God cannot fail in any word he has spoken — Chafer.

What assurance, then, does the Bible give us?

First, it assures us we can have eternal life now. And it further assures us we can know now that we have it. John the Beloved was inspired to write for these two reasons, and in that order: "But these are written, that ye might believe that Jesus is the Christ, the Son of God; and that believing ye might have life through his name" (John 20:31). "These things have I written unto you that believe on the name of the Son of God; that ye may know that ye have eternal life, and that ye may believe on the name of the Son of God" (1 John 5:13).

Assurance springs from knowing. Thus John employs the word *know* more than 25 times in his first epistle. We might call it the "Epistle of Assurance."

(1) We know if we keep His commandments. "And hereby we do know that we know him, if we keep his commandments" (1 John 2:3). Commandments here refer to the divine will. Are we set to do God's will? If that is our life's direction it is sound reason for assurance.

(2) We know if we keep His word. "But whoso keepeth his word, in him verily is the love of God perfected: hereby know we that we are in him" (v. 5).

His Word and His commandments are virtually the same. His will is revealed in His Word. Through His Word we learn His will. With our hearts we do His will. To learn and to do is to be assured. "He that doeth the will of God abideth forever" (v. 17).

(3) We know if we love the brethren. "We know that we have passed from death unto life, because we love the brethren" (3:14). Conversely, if we have hatred in our hearts, we know we don't know. "But he that hateth his brother is in darkness, and walketh in darkness, and knoweth not whither he goeth, because that darkness hath blinded his eyes" (2:11).

I like what Reuben Welch has to say about loving your brother:

> And don't forget that "brother" means fellow-Christian. Of course, we are to love all those who come into the circle of our world, but the place where love is to be going on is in the community of believers who share in the life of Christ. If love is not going on between us who know the Lord, what good is talk about people "out there"? It doesn't mean anything anywhere if it doesn't mean anything here between us in the fellowship.[1]

Love "in deed and in truth" is the springboard for genuine heart assurance.

Inside Information

A wonderful and meaningful plus for the believer is his *internal* assurance. This is the whispering of

---

[1]Reuben Welch, *We Really Do Need Each Other* (Nashville: Impact Books), p. 84.

God's Spirit to our spirit, and it is made possible through simple faith and obedience.

The Bible has a lot to say on the subject: "For as many as are led by the Spirit of God, they are the sons of God. . . . The Spirit itself beareth witness with our spirit, that we are the children of God" (Romans 8:14, 16). "And because ye are sons, God hath sent forth the Spirit of his Son into your hearts, crying, Abba, Father" (Galatians 4:6). "And he that keepeth his commandments dwelleth in him, and he in him. And hereby we know that he abideth in us, by the Spirit which he hath given us" (1 John 3:24).

G. Raymond Carlson writes:[2]

It is not easy to put into words just how this witness comes to us. It is not a witness in the flesh but in the spirit. John Wesley believed the witness of the Spirit was immediate. He thought of it as a believer's confidence that God had accepted him.

Often when a person accepts Christ, he sheds bitter tears of repentance and then experiences great joy. This is wonderful to behold. But we dare not base a matter as important as our salvation on emotions which rise and fall with the change of circumstances. The witness of the Spirit is more than inward joy, as blessed as such an experience is. The witness is a deep conviction that we have been received into the family of God — that we are sons of God.

* * *

But the witness of the Spirit, difficult to explain but none the less positive to experience, bears testimony with our spirit when we are born again. The great truth to which witness is given is that God is our Father and we are his children.

---

[2] G. Raymond Carlson, *Salvation*, pp. 57, 60.

Two plus two equals four—that is mathematics—count and see. Hydrogen and oxygen in proper proportion make water—that is science—taste and see. "Believe on the Lord Jesus Christ and thou shalt be saved"—that is salvation—try it and see. The last equation is just as true as the first two. In God's Word I read it; in the experience of my soul I know it.

On Gathering Grapes of Thorns

Our *external* ground for assurance is God's Word. Our *internal* ground for assurance is God's Spirit. But our *evidential* ground for assurance is our life: "Therefore if any man be in Christ, he is a new creature: old things are passed away; behold, all things are become new" (2 Corinthians 5:17).

A tree is known by its fruit, and so is the life of Christ. When the life of Christ is in us through the new birth it manifests itself: "He that saith he abideth in him ought himself also so to walk, even as he walked" (1 John 2:6). "Even so every good tree bringeth forth good fruit; but a corrupt tree bringeth forth evil fruit. A good tree cannot bring forth evil fruit, neither can a corrupt tree bring forth good fruit" (Matthew 7:17, 18).

We can assure ourselves that we indeed possess the life of Christ when our own lives have been transformed and we have become possessed of new desires. "In this the children of God are manifest, and the children of the devil: whosoever doeth not righteousness is not of God" (1 John 3:10).

The child of God is a citizen of another world: "Now therefore ye are no more strangers and foreigners, but fellow citizens with the saints, and of the household of God" (Ephesians 2:19). This means he no longer loves this present evil world. And when this is true, blessed assurance is born in his soul.

It is not difficult to make a test at this point, for John says: "If any man love the world, the love of the Father is not in him" (1 John 2:15). And James supports the same idea when he says: "Know ye not that the friendship of the world is enmity with God? whosoever therefore will be a friend of the world is the enemy of God" (James 4:4). Worldliness, therefore, is the enemy of assurance, while other-world mindedness ignites the glowing embers of full assurance.

How profoundly wonderful are the assurances God provides for His children when they simply meet the conditions. *Now* we can have the full assurance of faith. "Let us draw near with a true heart in full assurance of faith" (Hebrews 10:22). *Now* we can have the full assurance of understanding. "Being knit together in love, and unto all riches of the full assurance of understanding" (Colossians 2:2). And *now* we can have the full assurance of hope. "And we desire that every one of you do show the same diligence to the full assurance of hope unto the end" (Hebrews 6:11).

The nurse uses the pulse to determine blood pressure. The engineer watches the rise and fall of a drop of water in a glass tube to determine the pressure of steam in the boiler of a great locomotive. The movements of a small pointer on the dial of a barometer indicate what is happening in the vast area of atmosphere above us. Our spiritual life also has an index— "We know we have passed from death unto life, because we love the brethren" (1 John 3:14).[3]

---

[3]Ibid., p. 60.

9

When the Guilty Is Innocent

Antonio Santiago of Guadalajara, Mexico landed in jail for transporting 1,200 pounds of marijuana to the United States. But when Superior Court Judge Jack G. Marks of Tucson, Arizona learned the reason for Santiago's illegal act he delayed sentencing so the man could see his wife and child, and the charge of transporting marijuana was dropped.

What happened was this. Santiago had an 18-month-old girl who desperately needed surgery to correct a hole between two heart valves. He needed $10,000 and had been offered $5,000 to smuggle the marijuana into the U.S.

When Judge Marks, who had himself undergone open heart surgery, learned of Santiago's dilemma, he offered to pay for the child's surgery. "We're human beings first, and judges second," Marks said. "When I learned that the child might only live for another year or so, I called for the surgeon."

Marks paid travel expenses for the ailing child and her mother from Guadalajara and contacted the same Houston, Texas doctor who had operated on him in 1971.

The question is, was the guilty innocent? Should Santiago have paid for his crime? In view of the circumstances and out of hearts of compassion, most of us would side with Judge Marks.

But God had an even bigger problem than Marks. He had before Him in "court" the whole human family. And not a single person was guiltless. "For we have . . . proved both Jews and Gentiles, that they are all under sin; as it is written, There is none righteous, no, not one" (Romans 3:9, 10).

What was God to do about it? Could He, because of His great compassion, simply dismiss the charges? How could He, the holy God, justify unholy sinners and remain just himself? Is there any way to make the guilty innocent?

A North Dakota judge did it. But he incurred the wrath of the jury.

By telephone, a farmer had agreed to market 40,000 bushels of wheat to a certain grain elevator at $4 per bushel. On the basis of the verbal agreement the elevator manager contracted in turn to sell the 40,000 bushels for a fixed price.

The manager had the agreement with the farmer prepared in written form and called the farmer to come in and sign. And the farmer advised him he would be in within a few days.

This kind of negotiating is commonly done. But in a week wheat had jumped $2 per bushel in price, so the farmer backed out.

Now the elevator manager was in trouble because he had already contracted to sell the wheat before the price escalation. So he took the farmer to court.

Instructing the jury before the trial, the judge said: "If you can be persuaded beyond reasonable doubt, that a contract was entered into, whether signed or unsigned, you should bring a 'guilty' verdict."

The jury heard the case and immediately 11 of the 12 jurors found the farmer guilty. Soon to agree was the 12th jurist, who the first time around cast a "not guilty" vote. His reason was that he was sympathetic to the farmer since he had had a similar experience.

With one accord the jury agreed the farmer should make an $80,000 payment to the grain elevator manager. However, it was understood the judge could alter the amount. But the judge concurred.

Then came the shocker. After the jury was dismissed the judge reversed himself and let the farmer go scot-free without paying anything back!

You can imagine the anger of those jurors who were immediately up-in-arms over the breach of justice.

Some Judges, but Not God

It is to be conceded some judges are unjust, but God never. "For . . . God spared not the angels that sinned, but cast them down to hell, and delivered them into chains of darkness to be reserved unto judgment; and spared not the old world . . . and turning Sodom and Gomorrah into ashes condemned them with an overthrow, making them an example unto those that after should live ungodly" (2 Peter 2:4-6).

How then can God justify the ungodly? Job had the same question: "But how should man be just with God?" (Job 9:2). It is clear He cannot lightly overlook sin. "The Lord God . . . will by no means clear the guilty; visiting the iniquity of the fathers upon the children, and upon the children's children, unto the third and to the fourth generation" (Exodus 34:6, 7).

Grounds for Doing It

God found a way. Though He could not excuse our sin or simply close His eyes to our guilt, He, in infinite wisdom, conceived a plan by which He could make us who are guilty innocent and yet remain perfectly just himself. It is the way of substitution.

A substitute is one who takes the place of another. The fact is, we were all guilty of sin and justly deserved the death penalty: "The soul that sinneth, it shall die" (Ezekiel 18:4). The end of sin is always death: "And sin, when it is finished, bringeth forth death" (James 1:15). There is no exception to this rule. Remember the old adage: "Every rule has an exception, with the exception that every rule has an exception." In the case of sin, there is no exception to the required death penalty. The law is absolute and fixed. Let those who argue that "there are no absolutes" remember this.

The Scapegoat

There is a difference between sin and the sinner. Sin is an act or a condition. The sinner is a person. The solution to the problem is to be found in separating the sin from the sinner; for if the sin could be dealt with in justice apart from the sinner, the sinner could be returned to innocence.

How could it be done? A scapegoat was the answer. The Old Testament provides a beautiful insight. Aaron was instructed to take two goats and to cast lots upon them:

> One lot for the Lord, and the other lot for the scapegoat. And Aaron shall bring the goat upon which the Lord's lot fell, and offer him for a sin-offering. But the goat, on which the lot fell to be the scapegoat, shall be presented alive before the Lord, to make an atonement with him, and to let him go for a scapegoat into the wilderness. . . . And Aaron shall lay both his hands upon the head of the live goat, and confess over him all the iniquities of the children of Israel, and all their transgressions in all their sins, putting them upon the head of the goat, and shall send him away by the hand of a fit man into the wilderness: and the goat shall bear upon him all their iniquities unto a land not inhabited (Leviticus 16:8-10, 21, 22).

What Aaron was instructed to do was a prepicture of how, in actuality, God was going to solve the problem of making guilty sinners innocent. Jesus came to perform the function of the two goats. First, He became our scapegoat. Upon His blessed head God himself transferred the sin of the whole world. "For he hath made him to be sin for us, who knew no sin; that we might be made the righteousness of God in him" (2 Corinthians 5:21). That is what happened in Gethsemane.

But then came Calvary and the cross, where Jesus also fulfilled the role of the other goat. In Gethsemane all of man's sin fell upon Him, but at Calvary the penalty of that sin fell upon Him—and He died for it! And so Paul wrote: "While we were yet sinners, Christ died for us. Much more then, being now justified by his blood, we shall be saved from wrath through him" (Romans 5:8, 9).

That is how God arranged to make the guilty innocent. Man could by no device or means do it for himself. It was pure grace. "Being justified freely by his grace through the redemption that is in Christ Jesus" (3:24). "That being justified by his grace, we should be made heirs according to the hope of eternal life" (Titus 3:7).

Getting It for Yourself

What we want to know is how to get an "innocent" verdict for ourselves. We know we can't bribe the Judge or in any way buy ourselves off. How then do we get the advantage of what God has made available to us?

According to God's Word, there is only one way — faith. "Therefore we conclude that a man is justified by faith without the deeds of the law" (Romans 3:28). "And by him all that believe are justified from all things, from which ye could not be justified by the law of Moses" (Acts 13:39).

Faith takes what Jesus provided and makes it ours. By unbelief and disobedience Adam and Eve lost their innocence and became guilty. By the obedience of faith we lose our guilt and become innocent.

But there is a danger that we may think and speak too glibly about justification by faith. "Faith," according to the early Lutherans, "is a perturbing thing." And Tozer says:

> The faith of Paul and Luther was a revolutionizing thing. It upset the whole life of the individual and made him into another person altogether. It laid hold on the life and brought it under obedience to Christ. It took up its cross and followed along after Jesus with no inten-

tion of going back. It said goodby [sic.] to its old friends as certainly as Elijah when he stepped into the fiery chariot and went away in the whirlwind. It had a finality about it. It snapped shut on a man's heart like a trap; it captured the man and made him from that moment forward a happy love-servant of the Lord. It turned earth into a desert and drew heaven within sight of the believing soul. It realigned all life's actions and brought them into accord with the will of God. It set its possessor on a pinnacle of truth from which spiritual vantage point he viewed everything that came into his field of experience. It made him little and God big and Christ unspeakably dear. All this and more happened to a man when he received the faith that justifies.[1]

Now this is what James is talking about when he says: "Ye see then how that by works a man is justified, and not by faith only" (James 2:24). The faith that justifies is no mere passive acquiescence to God's Word. It must be tied to obedience like the unborn fetus is tied to its mother by the umbilical cord; else there is no means of life and sustenance.

Where faith and obedience are, there is also justification. For Paul says: "We have received grace . . . for obedience to the faith . . ." (Romans 1:5).

Dividends of Innocence

Innocence is itself a worthy goal. Who has not coveted the innocence of a tiny child? Through faith in Jesus we have it. Blessed innocence.

But innocence carries a bag of goodies which she bestows upon those who receive her.

Heading the list is *peace with God*. "There is no

---

[1]A. W. Tozer, *The Root of the Righteous* (Harrisburg, PA: Christian Publications, Inc., 1955), p. 46.

peace, saith my God, to the wicked" (Isaiah 57:21). While guilt floods our soul, peace can find no pleasant landing place. But let faith lay hold on the justification that is in Jesus and peace will flow in like a river. "Therefore being justified by faith, we have peace with God through our Lord Jesus Christ" (Romans 5:1).

We make a mistake, and so do the nations, when we make peace an end in itself. Peace is not a commodity to be bought, nor can it be gained by merely desiring it. Peace is a fruit. Plant the tree; it will produce the fruit. "Afterward it yieldeth the peaceable fruit of righteousness unto them which are exercised thereby" (Hebrews 12:11). "And the work of righteousness shall be peace" (Isaiah 32:17).

Another dividend is *access to God*. "Therefore being justified by faith . . . we have access . . . into this grace wherein we stand" (Romans 5:1, 2). How can the soul inhibited by guilt hope to gain audience with the holy God? No way! "If I regard iniquity in my heart, the Lord will not hear me" (Psalm 66:18). But the innocent find an open door. And they are bold as a lion to enter, for they know the scepter of acceptance is fully extended.

Add to this *rejoicing in hope*. "Therefore being justified by faith, we . . . rejoice in hope of the glory of God" (Romans 5:1, 2). While we are in sin we have no grounds for hope. The fellow who professes a hope of heaven and eternal life in this state has a false hope. Listen to Paul: "At that time ye were without Christ, being aliens from the commonwealth of Israel, and strangers from the covenants of promise, having no hope, and without God in the world" (Ephesians 2:12).

Hope is borne on the wings of innocence.

Furthermore, we are *free from condemnation.* "It is God that justifieth. Who is he that condemneth?" (Romans 8:33, 34). Condemnation is a heavy yoke. It is the natural result of evil. How wonderful then it is to know "there is therefore now no condemnation to them which are in Christ Jesus" (v. 1). The key is in the phrase "in Christ Jesus." Before we were justified we were *in sin.* In that state we were rightly under condemnation. But when we moved from *in sin* to "in Christ Jesus" the reason for our condemnation was removed. "He that believeth on him is not condemned" (John 3:18).

Last, but not least, we are *saved from wrath.* "Much more then, being now justified by his blood, we shall be saved from wrath through him" (Romans 5:9). All of the dividends previously mentioned have had a present application. We have peace with God *now.* We have access *now.* We rejoice in hope *now.* We are free from condemnation *now.* But this final dividend looks to the future—"we shall be saved from wrath." What a dividend this is! No more is there the awful prospect of wrath.

For the ungodly it is a different story: "A certain fearful looking for of judgment and fiery indignation, which shall devour the adversaries" (Hebrews 10:27). "For the great day of his wrath is come; and who shall be able to stand?" (Revelation 6:17). In that awful day His wrath will find expression: "In flaming fire taking vengeance on them that know not God, and that obey not the gospel of our Lord Jesus Christ: who shall be punished with everlasting destruction from the presence of the Lord, and from the glory of his power" (2 Thessalonians 1:8, 9).

But when the guilty are made innocent through the blood of Jesus, all fear of coming wrath is swept away. This is God's desire for all men: "As I live, saith the Lord God, I have no pleasure in the death of the wicked; but that the wicked turn from his way and live: turn ye, turn ye from your evil ways; for why will ye die . . .? (Ezekiel 33:11).

10

Hey God!

One of the remarkable Christian women of this century was Mama Foglio. Although she was only 4 feet 11 inches tall, she was a giant in God's kingdom.

It wasn't always that way, though. During her earlier years she was faithful to the religion of her forefathers. Her son, Frank, says, "She was always a meek, scared, shaky thing."

But then something happened. The Montecalvos, another Italian family like her own, a mother and father and 10 children, visited the Foglio home. They reported they had been filled with the Holy Spirit and God had directed them to seek out the Foglio family and teach them the Word of God.

What a battle followed! Mama Foglio rose to the situation. Suddenly she was defending her little family and her deep-rooted beliefs with all her might. Her faith was invincible as the battle with the Montecalvos raged in her home.

But the Montecalvos weren't about to be driven off. Fearlessly the mother of that little tribe began to preach the gospel. "Now all of you listen," she commanded. "I'm going to tell you exactly the way it is." And with that introduction she poured out the truth of God about Jesus, about being born again, and about being baptized in the Holy Ghost.

When this barrage was finished they launched another salvo: "Let us pray."

"How sneaky can you get?" writes Frank Foglio in his exciting book *Hey God.*[1] "You can't say no to a suggestion of prayer if you claim to be a professing Christian. They knelt down. There was nothing for us to do but to kneel also. So, we did. Now, you might think that we would close our eyes to pray. But we didn't; we wanted to see what they would do next. How did we know but that they might take off and fly around the room?

"While they prayed, they made funny noises under their breath, as though they were whispering some mumbo-jumbo language. My dad raged back and forth across the room cursing and calling God and everyone names. And during that prayer something happened that touched my heart. The old gentleman, the father of the Montecalvos, the one who led the pack to our home, raised his eyes heavenward and stretched out his arms to God and said, 'Oh, God, forgive them. Oh, God, open their minds and their hearts. Let the love of Christ saturate them.' " On and on he prayed.

Finally the prayer came to a halt with a loud "Amen." And the Montecalvos were gone.

But Mama Foglio had taken all she could. Dashing up the 17 steps of the stairs she ran to her bedroom, slammed the door, and began crying out to God.

---

[1]Frank Foglio, *Hey God* (Plainfield, NJ: Logos International, 1972), p. 19.

89

When it was all over she was a new woman. She had met God, and everybody knew it. The Holy Spirit had mightily filled her. Forever after she was to be a lighted candle blessing all she met.

Growing out of this revolutionizing experience was a most beautiful and tender relationship for Mama Foglio. Her heart was aglow with a new and overflowing love for her Heavenly Father and she spoke to Him in her simple and affectionate way: "Hey God! You know he dunno what to do. Look at him God. You love him. You gave Your Son to die for him. . . ."

At first thought we might be repulsed with the brashness of her "Hey God." But we need not be at all, for to Mama Foglio it was the same as saying, "Abba, Father."

"Abba, Father"

Twice Paul uses the expression "Abba, Father." "For ye have not received the spirit of bondage again to fear, but ye have received the Spirit of adoption, whereby we cry, Abba, Father" (Romans 8:15). "And because ye are sons, God hath sent forth the Spirit of his Son into your hearts, crying, Abba, Father" (Galatians 4:6).

The first to use the expression was Jesus himself: "And he said, Abba, Father, all things are possible unto thee . . ." (Mark 14:36).

What does it mean? *Abba* is a Syrian word intimating filial affection and respect and parental tenderness. Adam Clarke says it "seems to have been used by our blessed Lord, merely considered as a man, to show his complete submission to his Father's will.

And the tender affection which he was conscious his Father had for him."

"Father" is the Greek equivalent of the Syrian "Abba." The reason both words are used is that when the Jews became conversant with the Greek language through the Septuagint and through commerce with Roman and Greek provinces they often intermingled Greek and Roman words with their own language.

The Son first used the expression. Now, Paul says: "God hath sent forth the Spirit of his Son into [our] hearts," so that we along with His Son cry, "Abba, Father." How beautiful! To be enabled to say, "Abba, Father," out of our hearts is to be sons of God.

Sons by Adoption

Adoption is a process dating back to antiquity. It is defined as "the legal process by which a man might bring into his family, and endow with the status and privilege of a son, one who was not by nature his son or of his kindred".[2]

In the same publication the general legal idea of adoption is set forth:

> The custom prevailed among Greeks, Romans and other ancient peoples, but it does not appear in Jewish law.
>
> Three cases of adoption are mentioned: Moses (Exodus 2:10), Genubath (1 Kings 11:20), and Esther (Esther 2:7, 15), but it is remarkable that they all occur outside of Palestine—in Egypt and Persia; where the

---

[2] James Orr, ed., *The International Standard Bible Encyclopedia* (Grand Rapids: Wm. B. Eerdmans Publishing Co., rev. ed., 1930), vol. 1, p. 58.

practice of adoption prevailed. Likewise the idea appears in the New Testament only in the epistles of Paul, which were addressed to churches outside Palestine.

The motive and initiative of adoption always lay with the adoptive father, who then supplied his lack of natural offspring and satisfied the claims of affection and religion, and the desire to exercise paternal authority or to perpetuate his family. The process and conditions of adoption varied with different peoples. Among oriental nations it was extended to slaves (as Moses) who thereby gained their freedom, but in Greece and Rome it was, with rare exceptions, limited to citizens.

In Greece a man might during his lifetime, or by will, to take effect after his death, adopt any male citizen into the privileges of his son, but with the invariable condition that the adopted son accepted the legal obligations and religious duties of a real son.

In Rome the unique nature of paternal authority, by which a son was held in his father's power, almost as a slave was owned by his master, gave a peculiar character to the process of adoption. For the adoption of a person free from paternal authority, the process and effect were practically the same in Rome as in Greece. In a more specific sense, adoption proper was the process by which a person was transferred from his natural father's power into that of his adoptive father, and it consisted in a fictitious sale of the son, and his surrender by the natural to the adoptive father.

Surely Paul, being a Roman citizen from cosmopolitan Tarsus, was well acquainted with these processes of natural adoption. Yet to force upon his use of the word *adoption* some of the implications of its usage in one culture or another, may be to force on its Christian usage an unintended meaning.

For Paul it meant that manifestation of God's grace in Christ which brings men into the relation of sons to himself, and makes experientially real to them their sonship.

In the Book of Romans two opposites are in view: (1) the spirit of bondage, and (2) the spirit of adoption. The spirit of bondage relates to life under the Law. Three situations seem to be mingled in describing man in this condition: (1) that of a slave, (2) that of a minor under guardians appointed by his father's will, and (3) that of a Roman son under parental authority. In each case the relationship was marked by fear, which is generally the fruit of bondage.

The spirit of adoption is the extreme opposite. It engenders a relationship of love, whereby fear is dispelled and a beautiful father-son relationship is actualized. "There is no fear in love; but perfect love casteth out fear: because fear hath torment" (1 John 4:18).

Born or Adopted?

Due to our cultural concepts of adoption we are confronted with a problem. In our thinking, a son is recognized as a family member either because he was born into a family or because he was adopted into a family. He cannot fit both categories. However, this is not true of birth and adoption in the Christian scheme of things.

A Christian is both born and adopted. New birth and adoption are two sides of the same coin. The new birth is the process whereby we become children of God. While the will and work of God are involved in the new birth it cannot be effected apart from the will of man. In adoption the initiative rests entirely with our Heavenly Father: "And because ye are sons, God hath sent forth the Spirit of his Son into your hearts, crying, Abba, Father" (Galatians 4:6).

The International Standard Bible Encyclopedia has a helpful word: "The new birth defines especially the origin and moral quality of the Christian experience as an abstract fact, but adoption expresses a concrete relation of man to God."[3]

How does justification relate to adoption? In justification God's role is Judge; in adoption His role is Father. In justification our merciful Judge sets us, as prisoners, free. In adoption our Heavenly Father takes us into His bosom, giving us the Spirit of His Son and making us heirs of a goodly heritage.

And what of sanctification? How does it relate to adoption? Sanctification is an on-going process. Adoption is a finished act. Sanctification has to do with growth and cleansing. Adoption has to do with position and inheritance. The word *adoption* means to place as a son, and it carries the idea of an adult son who is possessed of certain rights and privileges.

The Best Is Yet to Come

Certain benefits accrue to us as a result of adoption in this life. Not the least of these is the inward witness that we are indeed the children of God. "The Spirit itself [himself] beareth witness with our spirit, that we are the children of God" (Romans 8:16). This witness in turn endows us with the peculiar ability to say, "Our Father," out of overflowing hearts.

History indicates that slaves were not permitted to use the terms *Abba* (father) or *Imma* (mother) in

---

[3] *Ibid.*

94

addressing their masters or mistresses. It is quite possible Paul had this in mind as he contrasted the "spirit of bondage" with the "Spirit of adoption." Under the "Spirit of bondage" men dared not call God, Father. But having escaped that state by grace, and having received the "Spirit of adoption," the reverse is true. Then it is most natural and meaningful to say, "Our Father."

And so we need not pass through this life as fatherless children or spiritual waifs. We have a Heavenly Father who delights in us and bestows upon us all the advantages of His fatherly concern. "If ye then, being evil, know how to give good gifts unto your children, how much more shall your Father which is in heaven give good things to them that ask him?" (Matthew 7:11).

Chastisement is part of the package too:

> If ye be without chastisement, whereof all are partakers, then are ye bastards, and not sons. Furthermore, we have had fathers of our flesh which corrected us, and we gave them reverence: shall we not much rather be in subjection unto the Father of spirits, and live? For they verily for a few days chastened us after their own pleasure; but he for our profit, that we might be partakers of his holiness (Hebrews 12:8-10).

But there is more to come: "Ourselves also, which have the firstfruits of the Spirit, even we ourselves groan within ourselves, waiting for the adoption, to wit, the redemption of our body" (Romans 8:23). The firstfruits of the Spirit are by no means the full harvest. They are only harbingers of the harvest. They are the earnest. The best is yet ahead.

And one of the blessed fruits awaiting the sons of

the Heavenly Father is redemption of the body: "Who shall change our vile body, that it may be fashioned like unto his glorious body, according to the working whereby he is able even to subdue all things unto himself" (Philippians 3:21). "We shall not all sleep, but we shall all be changed, in a moment, in the twinkling of an eye, at the last trump: for the trumpet shall sound, and the dead shall be raised incorruptible, and we shall be changed" (1 Corinthians 15:51, 52). That is the redemption of our bodies!

The Inheritance

In searching the Scripture passages relative to adoption, a correlation becomes evident between adoption and eternal inheritance. In fact, the great underlying purpose for adoption appears to be the ground for inheritance.

Israel's ground for inheritance was her relationship to Abraham. Every Jew was proud to proclaim, "Abraham is our father" (John 8:39). But the ground for our inheritance is that God is our Father.

Writing to the Romans, Paul says: "And if children, then heirs; heirs of God, and joint-heirs with Christ" (8:17). And to the Galatians he says: "Wherefore thou art no more a servant, but a son; and if a son, then an heir of God through Christ" (4:7).

But what is this inheritance our Heavenly Father intends to bestow upon us, His sons? It is doubtful if our fondest imaginations can even begin to perceive it. Yet our Father has permitted us to glimpse it. "In whom also, after that ye believed, ye were sealed with that Holy Spirit of promise, which is the earnest of our inheritance . . ." (Ephesians 1:13, 14).

Surely the natural mind cannot comprehend the inheritance at all. "But the natural man receiveth not the things of the Spirit of God: for they are foolishness unto him: neither can he know them, because they are spiritually discerned" (1 Corinthians 2:14).

Yet, the Holy Spirit himself is the earnest of the inheritance for the true sons of God. In giving us of His Holy Spirit, the Father is actually giving to us of himself. It is correct to say, God in this way shares of himself with us. And when this happens we say, "[It is] joy unspeakable and full of glory" (1 Peter 1:8).

But this is only a glimpse and a taste like the grapes of Eshcol were to Israel. It is only a small down payment of things to come. What shall it be when the Father shares all He is and has with us, His sons, eternally?

We should remember, too, that we are "heirs of God, and joint-heirs with Christ" (Romans 8:17). Christ, the Son, shall inherit all things: ". . . his Son, whom he hath appointed heir of all things" (Hebrews 1:2). And we shall inherit with Him!

11

Wholly Holy

Washing is an important part of living. Though the Bible doesn't say, "Cleanliness is next to godliness," it plainly teaches that cleanliness is godliness. "Jesus answered him [Peter], If I wash thee not, thou hast no part with me" (John 13:8).

What would living be like among people who did not wash themselves? Some missionaries found out. Seeking to evangelize a remote heathen tribe, they discovered that the tribe's idol religion forbade them to wash.

They asked the Lord for an opportunity to minister to some of the children, hoping to train the children in clean and Christian living, so they could become examples.

Then one day a young girl came to them requesting to learn to read and write. The missionaries told her she could come on one condition—that she wash herself. Hearing that, she turned and ran off.

But the missionaries continued to pray. Some weeks later the same girl showed up again with the same request. Learning that the requirements had not changed, she ran off again.

"Hang the large mirror near the door," the missionaries heard the Lord say. Not long after, they heard a loud scream and discovered the young girl had again returned but was frightened nearly senseless by the strange-looking something in the house.

Tenderly the missionaries assured her there was nothing dangerous in the house and they were finally able to lead her to the mirror. After a time of examination it dawned on her that whatever looked into the mirror also looked out. And she grew willing to wash and later became a Christian.

God wants us to be washed: "That he might sanctify and cleanse it [the Church] with the washing of water by the word, that he might present it to himself a glorious church, not having spot, or wrinkle, or any such thing; but that it should be holy and without blemish" (Ephesians 5:26, 27).

Bad Words

Holiness and sanctification are bad words to some people. To them they speak of straitjacket Christianity and outward, impossible piety. This is sad, for it has brought some of the Bible's great truths into disrepute and has shortchanged many of God's children.

We need to learn that no truth taught by the Bible is to be avoided, but that instead we should seek earnestly to understand it and experience the advantages of it.

Sanctification and holiness are not to be shunned like the plague. Why should we turn away from those things that yield the sweetest fruit? True holiness is the fountainhead of fullness of joy and gladness. "Thou hast loved righteousness, and hated iniquity; therefore God, even thy God, hath anointed thee with the oil of gladness above thy fellows" (Hebrews 1:9). And sanctification is the process that leads to this holiness.

Let's Get Things Clear

Terms tend to throw us. We hear the word *sanctification* and red lights begin to flash in our minds. We think of someone who loudly proclaims his entire sanctification and at the same time is contentious and cantankerous. Or we hear the word *holiness* and we have visions of drab clothing, dull living, and sanctimoniousness. How unfortunate!

Such corrupted concepts blind our eyes to beautiful truth and blight our experience. Therefore it is for our spiritual good health that we come to right understanding.

What does the Biblical word *sanctify* or *sanctification* mean? In simplest terms it means to separate. On the one hand, it indicates separation from sin, and thus it carries the idea of purification. "If a man therefore purge himself from these, he shall be a vessel unto honor, sanctified, and meet for the master's use, and prepared unto every good work" (2 Timothy 2:21). On the other hand, it indicates separation unto God, and thus it sets forth the idea of consecration.

We come very near the truth when we understand sanctification to be a *process*, and holiness to be a *state*. Holiness is derived from a word meaning "an awful thing," and it bespeaks the pristine purity of God himself. Thus, in the process of sanctification we are moving toward that state which is native to God.

There are two aspects to sanctification: (1) the positional, and (2) the experiential. Unless care is exercised it is easy to confuse the two.

Positionally, we are already sanctified: "By the which will we are sanctified through the offering of the body of Jesus Christ once for all" (Hebrews 10:10). In Christ our sanctification is an accomplished fact. "But of him are ye in Christ Jesus, who of God is made unto us wisdom, and righteousness, and sanctification, and redemption" (1 Corinthians 1:30).

But in us sanctification must be materialized. That is, it must be applied in a practical way to life. At the point of our believing on Jesus we are sanctified. In our day-by-day living for Jesus we are being sanctified.

Can the Leopard Change His Spots?

The obvious answer is no. No leopard has ever yet changed his spots. How then can the defiled and unclean sinner hope to attain the purity of God? No human wish, desire, or initiative by itself could ever gain such a goal. The initiative had to come from God —and it did. "In that day there shall be a fountain opened to the house of David and to the inhabitants of Jerusalem for sin and for uncleanness" (Zechariah 13:1).

There had to be a Sanctifier. Even as no filthy garment can cleanse itself, so no defiled sinner can cleanse himself. Only the clean can cleanse—and that is what happened.

For such a high priest became us, who is holy, harmless, undefiled, separate from sinners, and made higher

101

than the heavens; who needeth not daily, as those high priests, to offer up sacrifice, first for his own sins, and then for the people's: for this he did once, when he offered up himself (Hebrews 7:26, 27).

At the cross on Golgotha's hill, provision was made for cleansing away the sin of the whole world. And any guilt-ridden sinner who by simple faith appropriates the finished work of Jesus there can come away clean and sanctified.

An unknown poet said it well:

What though the accuser roar
O'er ills that I have done;
I know them well, and thousands more;
Jehovah findeth none.

His be the Victor's name
Who fought our fight alone;
Triumphant saints no honor claim;
Their conquest was His own.

By weakness and defeat,
He won the mead and crown;
Trod all our foes beneath His feet,
By being trodden down.

He hell, in hell laid low;
Made sin, He sin o'erthrew;
Bowed to the grave, destroyed it so,
And death by dying slew!

Bless, bless the Conqueror slain!
Slain by divine decree!
Who lived, who died, who lives again,
For thee, His saint, for thee.

102

How to Make It Work

In Christ we are sanctified. In experience we are being sanctified. Our difficulties rise out of this latter aspect. In a positive sense sanctification is faith at work. Jesus provided sanctification. Faith appropriates it. It doesn't just happen any more than an individual's salvation just happens. We must act. There are some things we must do. Paul lists them for us.

First is *knowing*. Sanctification like any other work of faith is based on knowing. "Knowing this, that our old man is crucified with him, that the body of sin might be destroyed, that henceforth we should not serve sin" (Romans 6:6).

Sin and uncleanness spring out of the old man, the old nature, the flesh. At the cross, in Jesus our Substitute, all of this died. This is not fiction; it is a fact. But only when we *know* this fact can faith lay hold upon it and apply it to our experience.

On a night in 1838 the slaves in Jamaica received the knowledge they were set free. It was then that they did a very meaningful thing. They made a large mahogany coffin and dug a grave. Into the coffin they threw the reminders of their former lives of slavery —whips, torture irons, coarse frocks and shirts, fragments of a treadmill, and handcuffs. Then the lid was securely fastened, and at midnight the coffin was lowered into the grave and buried, as the liberated slaves sang the doxology. Their knowing led to actual experience. So it is with us.

After knowing comes *reckoning*. "Likewise reckon ye also yourselves to be dead indeed unto sin, but alive unto God through Jesus Christ our Lord" (Romans 6:11). *Reckon* is a mathematical term mean-

103

ing to count, to compute, to take into account. Thus we are to count ourselves dead unto sin. We are not merely to play dead. By faith we are to recognize what in God's mind is fact—we are dead! Paul reckoned so. He said: "I am crucified with Christ" (Galatians 2:20). Appropriation brings realization. What faith appropriates experience attests.

Our reckoning is to be twofold. To count ourselves *dead to sin* is right and necessary; however, it is quite meaningless apart from also counting ourselves *alive unto God*. Death without prospect of new life is a dreadful thing, but it is not our lot. Jesus died unto sin once. Then He arose to live forevermore. "For in that he died, he died unto sin once: but in that he liveth, he liveth unto God" (Romans 6:10).

Paul identified himself with Christ in both death to sin and life unto God, and we must count ourselves in on the same identification. "I am crucified with Christ: nevertheless I live" (Galatians 2:20).

Sanctification is not only separation from sin and death. It is also separation unto righteousness and life.

There is one more step — *yielding*. "Neither yield ye your members as instruments of unrighteousness unto sin: but yield yourselves unto God, as those that are alive from the dead, and your members as instruments of righteousness unto God" (Romans 6:13). Note the negative and positive emphasis. The practical outworking of sanctification is related to human involvement, not just negatively, but both negatively and positively.

When sanctification is viewed only negatively, the result is disheartening bondage, and we cry in our despair, "O wretched man that I am! who shall deliver me from the body of this death?" (7:24). It is not enough to choose not to yield to sin. That is only half of the sanctification process. It is like trying to fly an airplane with one wing—disasterous. There must be positive action. The positive is: "Yield yourselves unto God" (6:13). The principle is: "Be not overcome of evil, but overcome evil with good" (12:21).

Koinonia Is the Key

The Greek word *koinonia* is translated by our words *fellowship* and *communion*. Today it is sometimes applied to certain groups intent on close and warm Christian relationships.

However, the apostle John uses the word primarily to bring into view an even higher relationship, that between man and his Maker: "And truly our fellowship [*koinonia*] is with the Father, and with his Son Jesus Christ" (1 John 1:3). And John indicates that this fellowship *(koinonia)* is the fountainhead of fullness of joy: "And these things write we unto you, that your joy may be full" (v. 4).

We need to sound the depths of that word *koinonia*, for within it is the glorious secret of true holiness. Essentially it means partnership, participation, intercourse, benefaction. It springs from another word *koinonos*, meaning a sharer. This is very helpful, for it indicates the idea of one sharing with another or two sharing a common thing, as in the marriage union, wherein two become one.

I think this was the burden of Jesus in His high-priestly prayer: "And for their sakes I sanctify myself, that they also might be sanctified through the truth. . . . That they all may be one; as thou, Father, art in me, and I in thee, that they also may be one in us" (John 17:19, 21).

You may say: "What has all of this got to do with sanctification and holiness?" The answer is, nearly everything! For John understood that by our genuine oneness and union with God, our partaking of God's own nature is made possible, which is the epitome of absolute holiness. Thus, through *koinonia* God's holiness is ours, for we are possessed of and one with that eternal life which is holiness by its very nature.

Koinonia Is Conditional

"If we say that we have fellowship [*koinonia*] with him, and walk in darkness, we lie, and do not the truth" (1 John 1:6). The requirement imposed upon us for maintaining the *koinonia* relationship is quite simple. There is a single condition—walk in the light. The reason is obvious: "God is light, and in him is no darkness at all" (v. 5). And Paul says: "What communion [*koinonia*] hath light with darkness?" (2 Corinthians 6:14).

Walking in the light is the ongoing process of sanctification, through which holiness is maintained. On the other hand, walking in darkness militates against holiness and undermines the foundations from whence fullness of joy springs.

So we had better understand what walking in the light and walking in darkness really mean. The two important words are *light* and *darkness*. Light is what God is.

Reuben Welch says: "God doesn't have any dark folds in His cloak. There is no deceit, no caprice, no trickery, no hypocrisy, no game-playing with God. He is light, is true, is pure — He is sincere. . . . God is a person of integrity—utterly. He is not hiding anything beneath the folds of His garment."[1] Darkness is the exact opposite. As light is the nature of God, so darkness is the nature of Satan. Darkness is evil, unrighteousness, impurity, and sin.

The crux of the matter is our walk; that is, the continuing direction of our life. If we walk in darkness there can be no continuing *koinonia*—it is impossible. "But if we walk in the light, as he is in the light, we have fellowship [*koinonia*]" (1 John 1:7).

Does this mean the Christian is wholly sanctified and sinlessly perfect? Not at all. But it does mean that the Christian who is concerned about *koinonia,* and discovers, by means of the light in which he walks, shades of darkness in his path, hastens to quit or escape that darkness. "If we say that we have no sin, we deceive ourselves, and the truth is not in us. If we confess our sins, [which is a part of walking in the light] he is faithful and just to forgive us our sins, and to cleanse us from all unrighteousness" (vv. 8, 9). That is sanctification.

Holiness is our objective. "Follow . . . holiness, without which no man shall see the Lord" (Hebrews 12:14). Sanctification is the means both to attaining and maintaining the desired end. "And the very God of peace sanctify you wholly; and I pray God your whole spirit and soul and body be preserved blameless unto the coming of our Lord Jesus Christ" (1 Thessalonians 5:23).

---

[1]Welch, *We Really Do Need Each Other,* p. 42.

12

No-cut Contract

Frankly, I'm a bit worried. My concern has been aroused by a *Reader's Digest* article (August 1976), "When Face to Face With Death." It was written by Sam Keen, based upon interviews with Elisabeth Kubler-Ross, M.D.

While the article can be a tremendous source of help and strength to some, I'm afraid it may generate a false sense of security for many.

Dr. Kubler-Ross gets the idea across that death need not be feared, for after all it is but an escape from earth's dread circumstances and an entry into beauty and bliss defying the imagination.

In support of her view she tells of a patient who, after being pronounced dead despite every conceivable effort at resuscitation, spontaneously came alive 3½ hours later. The woman told her of what happened while she was "dead." She had escaped her physical body, and while the medical team struggled to bring her back she watched the whole affair. She gave an accurate description of the resuscitation team, telling who was there, who wanted to abandon the effort, who wanted to keep trying, and even who cracked a joke to dispel the tension.

Since that time, Dr. Kubler-Ross has examined

many clear-cut cases of both religious and nonreligious people around the world. One had been dead over 12 hours. All had very identical experiences.

In her own words she says: "They virtually shed their physical bodies, as a butterfly comes out of a cocoon. They describe a feeling of peace, no pain, no anxiety. And they were perfect—completely whole."

She goes on to tell of a young man whose leg was severed in an auto accident. He floated over the accident scene, watching the rescue effort.

In all the cases their contentment was so profound that they resented, sometimes bitterly, the heroic attempts to revive them, "because they were returning to a dreadful existence—cancerous bodies, amputated limbs. Not one of them was afraid to die again."

And that's what concerns me. Is it safe to bank on the good doctor's inference that all have a common experience in dying, and that for all it is entry into a new form of existence far superior to the present life? The Bible's answer is "no."

We are wise to heed carefully Jesus' words on the subject, for He makes it clear that the fate of all is not the same: "And . . . the beggar died, and was carried by the angels into Abraham's bosom: the rich man also died, and was buried; and in hell he lifted up his eyes, being in torments, . . ." (Luke 16:22, 23). "Enter ye in at the strait gate: for wide is the gate, and broad is the way, that leadeth to destruction, and many there be which go in thereat: because strait is the gate, and narrow is the way, which leadeth unto life, and few there be that find it" (Matthew 7:13, 14).

Everybody craves security—especially beyond this life. Do we dare take a chance that Dr. Kubler-Ross' conclusions are right? If not, is there such a thing as genuine security which can be our lot now, and which will not miscarry at the moment of death?

A story from United States history can help us get our bearings. A wagon train was pressing its way westward across the plains. The trip had been unexpectedly pleasant, and the travelers were filled with anticipation of homesteading in Oregon and California. Then tragedy loomed on the horizon—a prairie fire! They looked with agonizing terror at the onrushing scourge of the western traveler. Fear ate at them as they studied the distant flames, fanned by a sturdy west wind, roaring hungrily toward them. And the cry arose, "We are lost; what shall we do?"

Watching the looming peril, a well-taught guide for the party sprang into action. Moving quickly, he went a few paces downwind of the wagon train and started several new fires in the dry grass. In minutes the wind carried the new fire along, leaving only the blackened earth in its wake.

Then came the guide's order: "Move right now into the place where the fire has already burned. Bring your children, your animals and your wagons."

Seeing the wisdom of the directive, the entire party hastened to obey, and they had no sooner found the place of security than the great fire approached only to die in its tracks as it reached the already burned ground.

The Bible teaches there is such a place of security spiritually; and it, like the wagon-train guide, points the way.

A Perfect Burn

Safety for the wagon train depended on the guide's success in preparing a place where the fire could not touch them. Had his fire-fighting device failed, or had he been unable to get his fire started, all would have perished.

Jesus, the Saviour, accomplished a perfect "burn." He prepared the "ground" for our assured security. "Wherefore he is able also to save them to the uttermost that come unto God by him, seeing he ever liveth to make intercession for them" (Hebrews 7:25). And to be more technical, He is the "ground" for our security.

The place of perfect security is in Christ Jesus. The Scriptures speak of this in two ways. In some instances they speak of us being *in Christ*. In other instances they speak of *Christ in us*. But in both cases the idea is set forth that our security is based on a vital relationship with Him.

"There is therefore now no condemnation to them which are in Christ Jesus" (Romans 8:1). "For the Lord himself shall descend from heaven with a shout, with the voice of the archangel, and with the trump of God: and the dead in Christ shall rise first" (1 Thessalonians 4:16).

"And if Christ be in you, the body is dead because of sin; but the Spirit is life because of righteousness. But if the Spirit of him that raised up Jesus from the dead dwell in you, he that raised up Christ from the dead shall also quicken your mortal bodies by his Spirit that dwelleth in you" (Romans 8:10, 11). "To whom God would make known what is the riches of the glory of this mystery among the Gentiles; which is Christ in you, the hope of glory" (Colossians 1:27).

Outside of Christ there is no security. He is the only safe place. "And a man shall be as a hiding place from the wind, and a covert from the tempest; as rivers of water in a dry place, as the shadow of a great rock in a weary land" (Isaiah 32:2).

Don't Abandon the Ship

Security for the believer is not an unconditional thing, John Calvin not withstanding. Calvin held the view that salvation was entirely God's doing and man had little or nothing to do with it. His doctrinal position was circumscribed by four basic concepts: (1) That fallen man is totally depraved and has nothing to commend him to God; (2) That lost man receives everything, including faith to be saved, directly from God; (3) That men who get saved have been divinely elected before the foundations of the world; and (4) That those whom God calls and regenerates are eternally secure, preserved unto final salvation.

From this view springs the idea that a person once saved is always saved.

Jacob Arminius held a somewhat different view. He believed that man's free will played a large role in his salvation and that human perseverance was necessary to avoid apostasy.

The two views have been set in array against each other for centuries. It is doubtful the conflict will be resolved this side of heaven. Both views have profound Biblical basis, and it is likely that each balances the other.

While Calvinism tends to breed false security,

especially when pressed to its extremes, Arminianism tends to breed insecurity. We want to and can avoid both false security and insecurity. And, after all, our security is not determined by the particular view we may hold but by our active, personal relationship to Christ Jesus.

Security is the sweet fruit of abiding. The place of security is provided. The abiding is our responsibility—and ours alone. Paul's advice to the centurion and soldiers aboard the troubled ship in the Adriatic Sea surely has a spiritual application: "Except these abide in the ship, ye cannot be saved" (Acts 27:31).

If we will concern ourselves with abiding in Christ, God will concern himself with keeping us. "Because thou hast kept the word of my patience, I also will keep thee ..." (Revelation 3:10). "Keep yourselves in the love of God, looking for the mercy of our Lord Jesus Christ unto eternal life" (Jude 21). "For I know whom I have believed, and am persuaded that he is able to keep that which I have committed unto him against that day" (2 Timothy 1:12).

Diagnosis and Prescription

Teachers and preachers are often victims of a subtle temptation to diagnose problems without prescribing a remedy. We must avoid this. We have pinpointed the idea that security springs from abiding, but the big question now is, what do we do to abide?

John is our source. In his Gospel he introduces the subject by telling us the unalterable need for abiding: "If ye keep my commandments, ye shall abide

113

in my love; even as I have kept my Father's commandments, and abide in his love" (John 15:10).

But in his first epistle he tells us *how to do it.* We abide by walking as He walked: "He that saith he abideth in him ought himself also so to walk, even as he walked" (1 John 2:6).

We abide by loving our brother: "He that loveth his brother abideth in the light. . . . We know that we have passed from death unto life, because we love the brethren. He that loveth not his brother abideth in death. Whosoever hateth his brother is a murderer: and ye know that no murderer hath eternal life abiding in him" (v. 10; 3:14, 15).

We abide by having His Word abiding in us: "I have written unto you . . . because ye are strong, and the word of God abideth in you, and ye have overcome the wicked one" (2:14).

We abide by doing God's will: "He that doeth the will of God abideth for ever" (v. 17).

We abide by retaining that which we have heard from the beginning: "Let that therefore abide in you, which ye have heard from the beginning. If that which ye have heard from the beginning shall remain in you, ye also shall continue in the Son, and in the Father" (v. 24).

We abide by having, and being taught by, the anointing: "But the anointing which ye have received of him abideth in you, and ye need not that any man teach you: but as the same anointing teacheth you of all things, and is truth, and is no lie, and even as it hath taught you, ye shall abide in him" (v. 27).

We abide by not sinning: "Whosoever abideth in him sinneth not" (3:6).

114

We know we abide by the Spirit He has given us: "And he that keepeth his commandments dwelleth in him. And hereby we know that he abideth in us, by the Spirit which he hath given us" (v. 24).

We abide by confessing Jesus: "Whosoever shall confess that Jesus is the Son of God, God dwelleth in him, and he in God" (4:15).

The Big "If"

We are secure *if.* . . . On the God-ward side the security is provided and positive: "And I give unto them eternal life; and they shall never perish, neither shall any man pluck them out of my hand" (John 10:28).

Little wonder then that Michael Horban can say with conviction, "We are eternally alive now." And Savonarola of Florence could cry with great assurance, "They may kill me, but they can never, never, never tear the living Christ out of my heart."

As far as God is concerned the "contract" is permanent. He cannot default.

But man can violate the provisions of the contract and invalidate it. The decision is his. Judas did it: "Judas by transgression fell, that he might go to his own place" (Acts 1:25).

"If" is the determining factor: "For if ye live after the flesh, ye shall die: but if ye through the Spirit do mortify the deeds of the body, ye shall live" (Romans 8:13). "For if God spared not the natural branches, take heed lest he also spare not thee. Behold therefore the goodness and severity of God: on them which fell, severity; but toward thee, goodness, if thou continue in his goodness: otherwise thou also shalt be cut off" (11:21,22).

In the hand of Jesus we are secure.

While guiding a party of climbers along a precipitous Alpine trail, a vicious crevasse was encountered. The Swiss guide leaped across the narrow chasm, then turned inviting his party to follow. The first man peered down the yawning gap, lost his courage, and turned back. "Look," ordered the guide, "see this hand? It has never yet let a man fall. Jump!"

With his eyes on the strong man, the climber leaped into space and was pulled to safety.

Jesus extends to all His nail-scarred hand and says, "See this hand? This hand has never failed a man yet. Trust me and you will be secure."

13

Breaking the Earth Barrier

Extending along 1250 miles of Australia's shoreline is the Great Barrier Reef, the most magnificent of the world's coral reefs. Though it follows the shoreline it is separated from it by a waterway or lagoon which forms a barrier between it and the open sea. The only way to the open sea from the mainland is to somehow escape the confining barrier.

Barriers like this are not uncommon to men. Until May 6, 1954 man, at least in recorded history, never had run a mile in 4 minutes. The reason — a very real psychological barrier. No one had ever done it; therefore, it could not be done. That is until an Oxford medical student named Roger Bannister came up with the idea he could do it. And he did it.

Payton Jordan and Bud Spencer writing in *Champions in the Making* commented:

> When Roger Bannister . . . broke through four minutes with a 3:59.4, he reduced the superlative to a level of simple mortal reality and removed a barrier which had thwarted many capable challengers for years. This barrier was psychological and was erected on a widespread impression that the feat was beyond the powers of human endurance.

As soon as this myth was removed, the four-minute mile was attacked and pierced so often and with such apparent ease that any time over four minutes was just too trifling to mention. . . . In almost no time the four-minute achievement was bettered 66 times by 26 men![1]

In aviation's infancy, as the speed of planes increased, a most dangerous and troublesome barrier was confronted. They dubbed it the "sound barrier" because it occurred as planes approached the speed of sound. In the experimental stages, before supersonic design, planes sometimes were crippled or torn apart by the strain resulting from extreme resistance at that point.

What a triumphant day it was when body design caught up with the speeds generated by the high-powered motors. That was a glorious new day for aviation.

Up Against It

Christians bump into barriers too. And there are big dividends for those who overcome them.

All of us are confined to mortal bodies, but we strain toward immortal ones: "For we know that the whole creation groaneth and travaileth in pain together until now. And not only they, but ourselves also, which have the firstfruits of the Spirit, even we ourselves groan within ourselves, waiting for the adoption, to wit, the redemption of our body" (Romans 8:22, 23).

Then there is the barrier between the earthly and

[1] Payton Jordan and Bud Spencer, *Champions in the Making* (Englewood Cliffs, N.J.: Prentice-Hall, Inc., 1968), p. 65.

the heavenly. We all come up against it: "As is the earthy, such are they also that are earthy: and as is the heavenly, such are they also that are heavenly. And as we have borne the image of the earthy, we shall also bear the image of the heavenly" (1 Corinthians 15:48, 49).

Another is the barrier between corruption and incorruption: "For this corruptible must put on incorruption, and this mortal must put on immortality" (v. 53).

Identify the Barriers

Scripture pinpoints the barriers between us and God's ultimate intention for us. The obvious one is sin. It stops us cold in our tracks, hiding God's face, and blocking the entrance to His paradise. But we have already discussed in previous chapters how Jesus, God's Son, by His sacrificial death overturned that barrier, making possible our spiritual reunion with God.

Yet while we who have been born again are seated with Christ in the heavenlies, as God sees things, we are very much confined to earth and separated from heaven in our experience.

The inspired hymnist had this in mind when he wrote:[2]

I have a heritage of joy
That yet I must not see;
The hand that bled to make it mine
Is keeping it from me.

---

[2] J. W. Van Deventer, "We Shall Shine as the Stars."

To aid our understanding, Paul gave us a key: "Therefore we are always confident, knowing that, whilst we are at home in the body, we are absent from the Lord" (2 Corinthians 5:6). He saw that our bodies are the barriers standing between us and our being present with the Lord.

Thus we conclude the final barrier to our eternal state is our earthly body. The evidence for this is abundant: "Now this I say, brethren, that flesh and blood cannot inherit the kingdom of God; neither doth corruption inherit incorruption" (1 Corinthians 15:50). "We are confident, I say, and willing rather to be absent from the body, and to be present with the Lord" (2 Corinthians 5:8).

There are also celestial bodies, and bodies terrestrial: but the glory of the celestial is one, and the glory of the terrestrial is another. There is one glory of the sun, and another glory of the moon, and another glory of the stars; for one star differeth from another star in glory. So also is the resurrection of the dead. It is sown in corruption, it is raised in incorruption: it is sown in dishonor, it is raised in glory: it is sown in weakness, it is raised in power: it is sown a natural body, it is raised a spiritual body. There is a natural body, and there is a spiritual body. And so it is written, The first man Adam was made a living soul; the last Adam was made a quickening spirit. Howbeit that was not first which is spiritual, but that which is natural; and afterward that which is spiritual (1 Corinthians 15:40-46).

Metamorphosis

Butterflies were not always butterflies. First they were ugly worms. What happened? A phenomenal change had to take place. And when it did, in God's own time and way, those ugly worms were glorified.

A similar thing is on the agenda for us: "For our conversation is in heaven; from whence also we look for the Saviour, the Lord Jesus Christ: who shall change our vile body, that it may be fashioned like unto his glorious body" (Philippians 3:20, 21).

Change must happen. Our present bodies are mortal, corruptible, earthly. They are limited by space, time, and matter. They are burdened with disease, deterioration, and death. How and when shall we escape this awful barrier into the freedoms of the eternal glorious state? "Behold, I show you a mystery; We shall not all sleep, but we shall all be changed, in a moment, in the twinkling of an eye, at the last trump: for the trumpet shall sound, and the dead shall be raised incorruptible, and we shall be changed" (1 Corinthians 15:51, 52).

What About the Eternal State?

God wants us to know some things about it, first to whet our appetites, and second to stimulate our preparation. Remember Paul's prayer in Ephesians 1:18: "That ye may know what is the hope of his calling." And recall John's inspired insight: "And every man that hath this hope in him purifieth himself, even as he is pure" (1 John 3:3).

Some may think it a waste of time trying to comprehend our glorified state. A. W. Tozer has a good answer for them:

> It has been cited as a flaw in Christianity that it is more concerned with the world to come than with the world that now is, and some timid souls have been fluttering about trying to defend the faith of Christ against these accusations as a mother hen defends her chicks from the hawk.

Both the attack and the defense are wasted. No one who knows what the New Testament is about will worry over the charge that Christianity is otherworldly. Of course it is, and that is precisely where its power lies.[3]

So let's discover all we can about what lies ahead for us Christians. It will make things easier for us now. "Jesus, . . . for the joy that was set before him endured the cross" (Hebrews 12:2). Likewise Moses "endured, as seeing him who is invisible" (11:27).

Glory—The Loaded Word

What we have been talking about is called, in theological jargon, *glorification*. But a word like that, while it sounds nice and may have an exciting ring to it, needs taking apart so we can get at the meat of it.

At its base is the curious word *glory*. We need to do a bit of sorting, for several Hebrew and Greek words are translated into the English word *glory*. While the word is applied to men and things on the earthly scene in numerous ways, our concern is to discover what it means when applied to God and to those who partake of His glory, particularly in their eternal state.

Glorification means to be endowed with God's glory. But what is glory? What is this thing that happens to us upon escaping the earthly barrier? What makes it so worthy of pursuit?

---

[3]A. W. Tozer, *Of God and Men* (Harrisburg, PA: Christian Publications, Inc.), p. 127.

What Did Moses See?

Once Moses prayed, "I beseech thee, show me thy glory" (Exodus 33:18). God's answer was somewhat of a revelation of the word's meaning. We get the sense that God and His glory are almost synonymous, and that His glory is simply and profoundly the outshining of His magnificent being: "I will make all my goodness pass before thee" (v. 19). His goodness and His glory are one: "And it shall come to pass, while my glory passeth by, that I will put thee in a cleft of the rock, and will cover thee with my hand while I pass by" (v. 22). His glory and He himself are one.

It is noteworthy that Moses could not see all of God, only a passing glimpse, like the vapor trail of a far-off jet-powered plane. The reason, given was: "There shall no man see me, and live" (v. 20). The earth barrier was the obstacle. Moses was yet a mortal earthling. That barrier had to be overcome before he could bear the fullness of His glory.

More Light

In the New Testament too, glory is related to God's image: "But we all, with open face beholding as in a glass the glory of the Lord, are changed into the same image from glory to glory, even as by the Spirit of the Lord" (2 Corinthians 3:18). That's what God is after. Nothing less will satisfy Him. He is set on seeing himself in His sons. And not for some selfish reason, but for our glory.

Watch a father gazing intently into the face of his son. What is he looking for? One thing—traces of himself. And what fulfillment comes when he finds it. So it is with God.

Glorification, then, is the ultimate of God's bestowal of himself upon His children. "For whom he did foreknow, he also did predestinate to be conformed to the image of his Son, ... and ... them he also glorified" (Romans 8:29, 30).

Let it be said here reverently, glory is the stuff of which God is made. It is the outshining of His personality. Glorification is the apex of personality infusion: "I in them, and thou in me, that they may be made perfect in one" (John 17:23).

Glory is the substance with which Jesus was rich before He became poor: "Though he was rich, yet for your sakes he became poor, that ye through his poverty might be rich" (2 Corinthians 8:9). Sin made us all paupers: "For all have sinned, and come short of the glory of God" (Romans 3:23). But Jesus came and was made sin for us that He might make us rich with His glory. Glorification is the bestowal of heaven's riches upon us.

And glory is heaven's medium of exchange. "For our light affliction, which is but for a moment, worketh for us a far more exceeding and eternal weight of glory" (2 Corinthians 4:17).

Preview of Glory

Definition of the unseen defies the best imagination. We will never fully understand glorification until we experience it. But testimonies of eyewitnesses do help. Peter, James, and John "were eyewitnesses of his majesty" (2 Peter 1:16). Luke writes: "They saw his glory" (Luke 9:32). And

Matthew records: "[He] was transfigured before them: and his face did shine as the sun, and his raiment was white as the light" (Matthew 17:2).

What a preview of restored glory! And what an impact it had on the three who witnessed it. They were afraid. They fell on their faces. They were transfixed. They had glimpsed God shining through as He would again when Jesus' earthly mission was ended. "And now, O Father, glorify thou me with thine own self with the glory which I had with thee before the world was" (John 17:5).

In our glorification Jesus will share His glory with us: "Father, I will that they also, whom thou hast given me, be with me where I am; that they may behold my glory, which thou hast given me" (v. 24). "It doth not yet appear what we shall be: but we know that, when he shall appear, we shall be like him; for we shall see him as he is" (1 John 3:2). That is glorification.

A Foretaste

Eshcol's grapes were a foretaste of Canaan's glory for Israel. The Holy Spirit is a foretaste of heaven's glory for us. "That Holy Spirit of promise, which is the earnest of our inheritance until the redemption of the purchased possession, unto the praise of his glory" (Ephesians 1:13, 14).

Now, through the Holy Spirit, glory touches our spirits and transforms them into the very image from whence that glory springs. And we cry with Peter, it is "joy unspeakable and full of glory" (1 Peter 1:8).

The more we permit the Holy Spirit to expose us to the glory now, the more our present transformation.

Little wonder then that Moses' face shone with such glory when he came down from Sinai that men could not bear to look upon him.

What then shall it be when we stand in His presence and partake of the glory that shall be revealed?

We shall shine as the stars of the morning
With Jesus the crucified One
We shall rise to be like Him forever
Eternally shine as the sun.